Copyright Notice ....

The Key Players ....

Potted History ....

Walk 1 - Piazza del Duomo to Piazza della Signoria 8

Walk 2 - Piazza della Signoria to the Pitti Palace 74

Walk 3 - The Uffizi 121

Walk 4 - The Accademia 141

Walk 5 - A view across the Arno 175

Other Tuscan Gems 183

Copyright Notice

Strolling Around Florence by Irene Reid

ISBN: 9781520479316

The Key Players

Florence has a LOT of history, and it will help to just be familiar with the main characters who you will meet over and over again as you explore.

The Medici

This is the family who more or less ruled Florence for several centuries. They eventually fizzled out in the eighteenth century, but here are their stars:

Cosimo the Elder

Cosimo Vecchio or Cosimo the Elder was the first of the Medici family to wield real power in Florence. He was a very, very successful banker who used his money and connections to virtually rule Florence in all but name – even though Florence was technically a democracy. However he was seen as just too powerful by some of the other Florentine families and was imprisoned and then exiled to Padua on very dubious charges. From Padua he pulled his vast fortune out of Florence and influenced many of the other wealthy families to do the same. Florence had no choice but to ask him back and he was soon in even more control of the city. Despite this he was generally seen as a good influence, as he spent his wealth in securing Florence and in beautifying it.

Lorenzo the Magnificent

Lorenzo was the grandson of Cosimo the Elder. He was a ruthless leader but also loved the arts - whatever Cosimo the Elder and Cosimo I didn't commission, Lorenzo probably did.

Cosimo I

Cosimo I was on a distant branch of the Medici family, but when the main line withered out, he inherited the title of Grand Duke of Tuscany. He increased the Medici family's power which they held onto over several centuries. He was

3

the most powerful of the Medici clan and was responsible for many of the sights you will see in Florence.

You might ask why he is called Cosimo I when they were other Cosimos before him. It is because he was the first Grand Duke of Tuscany.

Dante

Dante was a poet who was exiled from Florence due to political shenanigans. He is famous for his epic poem "The Divine Comedy", and his unrequited love for Beatrice, his teenage love.

Brunelleschi

Brunelleschi was the architect genius who figured out how to build the huge dome of Florence Cathedral and many other buildings you will see.

Michelangelo, Da Vinci, Giotto, Raphael, Botticelli, Caravaggio....

The list goes on and on. So many of the famous Italian artists started in or flocked to Florence where they were encouraged and commissioned by the Medici and other key families in Florence.

Pazzi, Strozzi....

These are the "other" Florentine families. They were never as powerful as the Medici, but gave them a good run for their money.

Potted History

The first settlers in this area of Tuscany were the Etruscans who arrived here about 800 BC. With safety in mind they built their town on top of a nearby hill - their settlement was the neighbouring town we now call Fiesole.

Florence itself came into being much later in 59 BC, and started out as a retirement area for Roman soldiers. The soldiers didn't show too much imagination when they returned to civilian life - they built their new home in a grid pattern, just like an army camp. The new town of Florentia was ideally positioned for success, as it lay between Rome and its provinces to the north.

When the Roman Empire started to convert to Christianity Florence got its first martyr, Saint Miniato who you will read about on walk 5. By the time of the Holy Roman Empire, Florence was already an important city state – although nearby Lucca was the capital of the region. Unfortunately for Lucca Grand Duke Ugo decided to move house to Florence, and of course the seat of power went with him. Consequently Florence became rich and powerful, and exploded with art and architecture.

Guelphs and Ghibellines

Italy was politically split between supporters of the Emperor called Ghibellines, and supporters of the Pope called Guelphs. In Florence this division went even further due to a jilted bride in 1215. Two of the most powerful families in Florence were to be joined by a wedding, but the groom decided he didn't like his bride and left her standing at the altar. The Bride's family responded in spectacular fashion by murdering the groom. The other families of the city split into two camps, which happened to run more or less along the same lines as their political leanings. So Florence was split into Guelph and Ghibelline families.

The two factions fought and killed each other for generations, and whenever one side won, the other would be kicked out of Florence. However the exiles generally returned to resume the battle. Finally the Guelphs gained the upper hand and held onto power in 1270.

Politics and internal disputes didn't stop the rollercoaster of success. Florence, backed by the powerful gold Florin, spread its financial influence across Europe, and back home the merchant families and guilds held the reins of power.

The Medici

The top families of Florence were the Medici family, the Pazzi family, and the Strozzi family – you will read about their various confrontations through the walks. Regardless of their political ambitions, all three families were lovers of arts and architecture, and encouraged the artists who flocked to Florence in the Renaissance.

Technically Florence was a democratic republic, but the Medicis held the reins of power except during two periods of exile. Eventually the Medicis became the hereditary dukes of all Florence and its subject cities. Only little Lucca maintained its independence.

Like many ruling families the Medici had problems propagating the line and finally withered out in 1737. The Austrian crown took over. Later France annexed Tuscany, at least until Napoleon was defeated. The Austrians returned and only in 1859 did Tuscany join Italy. For a dizzy few years Florence was the capital, but Rome soon stepped up and took over. Florence then turned its attention back to trade and industry.

It was invaded by the Germans in WWII when Italy decided to switch sides – the Germans destroyed so much and killed so many as they retreated. Since then Florence has become a mecca for tourists and of course for art lovers.

Get Ready

Decide if you want to buy a Firenze Card. It's expensive, but if you are planning to visit all the sights on these walks you will be better off buying one. Not only do you no longer have to judge if it's "worth" going into a museum, you get to skip the very long queues. You can buy it at any of the tourist offices, or online before you travel at:

http://www.firenzecard.it/

Using the card is not quite as simple as the website implies. It only lets you into each "sight" once, which means that they have to keep track of its use. So in most places you visit you will still have to hand your card over to register your visit and get a receipt – which involves finding the right desk and perhaps a small queue. However it is faster than the normal queue especially for the major sights.

Before you set out to explore you might also want to check the opening hours of museums in Florence. The tourist office will supply you with a handy flyer with all the opening times on it.

The Maps

There are maps sprinkled all through the walks to help you find your way. If you need to check where you are at any point during a walk, always flip back to find the map you need.

Pace Yourself

Florence is brimming over with art and history, and it's very tempting to try to see absolutely everything. But if you do, you might suffer sensory overload and find you can't face another museum or painting.

So try to pick out what you most want to see before you set out, and then if you feel you can "take a bit more" dip into the many other items mentioned in the walks. If you do reach overload, then do as the title says, stroll around, and just enjoy Florence.

You should try to see the following "Must Sees":

Walk 1 - The Cathedral, The Baptistery, The Campanile, The Bargello, Santa Croce

Walk 2 - Palazzo Vecchio, Ponte Vecchio

Walk 3 - The Uffizi

Walk 4 - The Accademia, Medici Chapels, Santa Maria Novella

Walk 5 – The view

Walk 1 - Piazza del Duomo to Piazza della Signoria

Clockwatching

Be aware that The Bargello Museum which is covered on this walk and is a "must see", is only open until 14:00.

The Walk

This walk starts in the main square, Piazza del Duomo. This map shows you where everything is, but the order you visit each sight depends on queues and timing, so there is no prescribed route round it, other than where you start and where you exit.

This square gets very, very crowded so if you can, try to get here as early as possible, to give yourself time to explore the square itself before the masses arrive. It's a very good idea to have a look at the Baptistery exterior first - you will find its gorgeous doors seven deep with people most of the day.

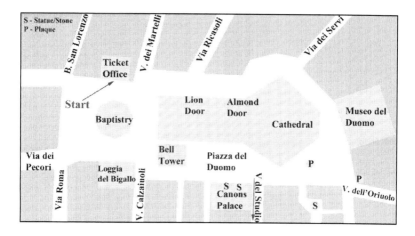

Piazza del Duomo – Tickets

Even if you have bought a Firenze card, you still need to go to the ticket office at Piazza San Giovanni 7 to get your "receipt". You need to show your receipt at the Cathedral Dome, the Campanile and the Crypt – so don't lose it!

To find the ticket office, stand facing the Baptistery with the Cathedral directly behind it. The ticket office is just behind the column topped with a cross, which you can see diagonally on your left. The ticket office door has a little statue above it. Show your Firenze card and you will be given your receipt.

You will probably want to visit all of the Cathedral Dome, the Cathedral, the Campanile, and the Baptistery. The opening hours differ slightly with the Cathedral opening last. So the order you visit them will depend on your start time.

Baptistery Exterior

The baptistery is not as famous as the cathedral but is spellbinding.

The first baptistery on this spot was probably built from the remains of Roman buildings which stood nearby. One theory says that part of the foundations came from the remains of a nearby Temple to Mars; however no-one really knows for sure exactly when it was built.

By the fifth century the baptistery had taken on its characteristic octagonal shape – the number eight represents rebirth in Christian symbolism. At that time it was surrounded by old Roman tombs which have now all been removed and are in museums or buried in cemeteries.

The baptistery you see today is still one of the oldest buildings in Florence, from the eleventh century, which is really just out of the dark ages. Legend says that the marble used came from Fiesole up on a nearby hill, a town that Florence defeated at the start of the tenth century.

Walk around the outside first to see the three sets of bronze doors decorated with intricate sculptures. They were done by master sculptors Pisano and Ghiberti – Pisano did the South doors and Ghiberti the North and East doors. The North and South doors each have 28 panels, and the East doors just 10.

South Doors

Once you have had a look at the doors themselves, take time to glance at the column on the right hand side. You will see an etched rectangle. This is the definitive measure of the "Lombard foot" used by merchants trading with Florence. The Lombard foot was standardised by Luitprando, a King of Lombardy in the eighth century.

There is also evidence of the building's Roman past which few tourists know about. It lies next to the South doors and you can find it if the renovations are completed when you visit. If the Baptistery is still shrouded in scaffolding, you will have to leave it for another trip. Face the South doors and walk a little to the left. Before you reach the West side of the Baptistery, look down and you will see an old Roman tombstone built into the wall.

North Doors

It took Ghiberti 21 years to complete the North doors which show the life of Jesus. You could spend a long time just gazing at each panel trying to identify the characters and the story portrayed.

At the moment the panels are not as eye-catching as the gold panels of the East Doors, but the original North Doors are being restored and it has been discovered that the panels are gilded just like the East Doors. So perhaps once the originals are back to their gleaming pristine state, the copies will also be gilded to match.

The East Doors

Ghiberti was asked to do the East doors after completing the North doors. They took 27 years and they show scenes from the Old Testament. When Michelangelo first saw the East doors, he proclaimed them to be the Gates of Paradise. What made them so special? Ghiberti used the revolutionary technique of perspective to give the panel's depth and realism, so that we can see a background and a foreground.

You will probably look at the Gates of Paradise most. From top left and reading across like a book, the scenes are:

- Adam and Eve
- Cain and Abel
- Noah
- Abraham
- Isaac with Esau and Jacob
- Joseph
- Moses
- The fall of Jericho
- David
- Solomon and the Queen of Sheba

They are all dramatic scenes, but personal favourites are Moses, and the Fall of Jericho.

Also there is a self-portrait of the artist himself, Ghiberti. He is on the left hand door between the third and fourth panel down – see the arrow on the picture below.

Of course these aren't the real doors – they are far too precious to leave to the elements and are in the Museum del Duomo, which must make you want to visit it.

The columns which stand on either side of the Gates of Paradise were pinched from Majorca by the Pisans when they invaded that island to rescue it from the invading Saracens. They gave them to Florence as a thank-you for guarding the city whilst they were at sea – like neighbours keeping an eye on the house whilst you go on holiday.

You might wonder why the baptistery is a separate building from the Cathedral. The reason is quite simple, in early medieval times, no-one was allowed inside the cathedral who was not baptized.

The Cathedral Exterior

Officially the Cathedral is called the Basilica di Santa Maria del Fiore but the locals call it Il Duomo – The Dome. It's one of the most iconic cathedrals you will see anywhere, instantly recognisable by its huge red dome.

Stand in front of the three huge bronze Cathedral doors and have a look at the exterior of the Cathedral before venturing in.

When Florence started to become a major power in Italy, its existing cathedral, Santa Reparata, was crumbling away, and was just too tiny for the exploding population. So a new cathedral was commissioned to replace it, the architect Cambio designed it, and the first stone was laid in 1296.

They actually constructed the new cathedral around Santa Reparata, and the old cathedral was still in use until it was finally no longer needed, and then demolished. Work on the new cathedral did not exactly race along - it took 140 years to complete.

The Wool Merchant's guild, which was one of the wealthiest in the city, was tasked with moving the job along in the fourteenth century as things had come to a grinding halt. They asked the experienced architect and artist Giotto to step in - and he designed the Campanile (bell tower) which you see standing on the right hand side of the Cathedral. When Giotto died Andrea Pisano from Pisa took over and kept things ticking along, and by 1419 only the dome was missing.

That proved to be a bit of a problem, because the space it had to cover would make it the largest dome ever built, and no-one knew how to do it. Suggestions included building a huge column in the middle to hold it up, and my personal favourite involved filling the cathedral with a pile of dirt to hold it up while it was constructed – but cunningly to put lots of coins in the dirt. When the dome was complete, the city's poor would be invited in to find the money, and clear the soil as they did so.

The problem was solved by Filippo Brunelleschi. He had studied the Pantheon in Rome which also has a huge dome, and he figured out how the Romans did it. He built two domes, one inside the other, to make the whole thing much lighter. He added internal rings of stone, like the hoops on a barrel, to stop the dome bulging out and collapsing under its own weight. Finally his workers laid the bricks in a herringbone pattern, not in straight line - you can see that pattern if you climb up inside the dome. All these measures were enough to stop the Dome collapsing in on itself. While he was at it, he also solved the problem of how to get all the heavy materials up there in the first place, he designed a crane!

The dome was finally completed in 1436, and on March 25th of that year the Pope arrived to consecrate the new cathedral. Brunelleschi's dome used to be the largest in the world. It is now the thirteenth largest, but is still the largest brick-built dome in the world. It took four million bricks to build it. It was seen as a wonder of the age.

The builders were also asked to maintain the style used by other older buildings on the square. The colourful marble facing and its myriad of decorations took a long time to complete – not until 1887. Progress wasn't exactly helped by the fact that a lot of the decorations were already in place but dismantled in 1587, by order of the Medici family who were in power at the time. They thought the façade was just too old-fashioned and a fresh start was ordered. So the decor was stripped.

You can see some of those old statues in the Museo del Duomo - others made it as far as the Louvre in Paris. Having stripped the cathedral no progress was then made, and the façade was left bare until the nineteenth century. Finally work began again in 1876 and took only two years to finish.

Have a look at the main doors – they are decorated with scenes from the Madonna's life. Near the top of the façade stand the twelve apostles, and further up you can see busts of Florence's many artists. In the central portal you can see a statue of Santa Reparata, whose church was removed to make way for the cathedral.

The cathedral's name translates as the Basilica of Saint Mary of the Flowers, so it's fitting that one of the panels on the right hand side doors shows The Annunciation, with Mary being given a flower from the Archangel Gabriel as he breaks the startling news about her unexpected pregnancy. You will see that scene often on your exploration of Florence as it's a favourite of all the artists.

Saint Zenobius

Don't ignore the column with the cross on top which stands beside the Baptistery near the ticket office.

Florence's first bishop was Saint Zenobius, who performed many miracles including several resurrections. His final miracle occurred as his remains were being transferred from his original tomb in San Lorenzo to Santa Reparata in chilly January. The bier carrying his remains brushed against an elm tree which immediately burst into flower. The column commemorates that miracle and if you look at the panel on the column you see the tree in full flower.

The saint's remains are now in an urn in a silver shrine inside the Cathedral. Before you go in, spot the statue of a bearded man holding a mitre and crook to the right of the Cathedral door - that's Saint Zenobius, keeping an eye on his column

The Lion Door

Now stand facing the front of the Cathedral and go down the left hand side. The first ornate door you pass is the Lion Door of which there is a legend.

16

In the fifteenth century, Anselmo from Florence had a phobia of lions and had nightmares every night about them. The doctor suggested that he should visit this door and push his hand into the mouth of one of the guarding lions to conquer his fear. Anselmo took a long time but finally summoned up the courage to try it. He placed his shaking hand into the mouth of one of the lions, but unfortunately a scorpion was nesting there and stung him. Anselmo dropped dead from the shock.

Continue down this side of the cathedral to reach the Dome entrance.

The Cathedral Dome

The Cathedral Dome is the first of the sights to open. The entrance is via the Cathedral's Almond Door – when you get there you will probably see a queue already forming! There will be two queues, a very small one for Firenze ticket holders and one for the rest of the world – remember you need to get your receipt before you start queuing.

The Almond door you are standing outside is the prettiest of the Cathedral's side doors. It gets its name because the panel above the door depicts the Annunciation, with Mary enclosed in an almond shaped background.

While you wait to get in, try to spot the bull's head which is above the door to the left. Like a lot of statuary in Florence there are legends. This one has two stories attached to it. The first one says it commemorates the animals that helped to construct the cathedral by carrying the heavy stones. The other is that a stonemason was having an affair with a baker's wife, but they were caught by the baker, charged with adultery and forced to separate. In Italian lore, horns imply that a man's wife is being unfaithful, so the stonemason put this bull up to gaze at the baker's shop and mock him.

The climb spirals up and around inside the dome walls, and of course it takes an effort to get up there. As you climb, remember to have a look at the brickwork for the "herringbone" pattern which Brunelleschi used to distribute the Dome's weight.

Eventually you will exit the walls to walk around the inside of the dome.

The Dome

Have a look at the dome frescoes before the last climb to reach the top. Unfortunately the authorities have ringed the walkway with a grubby Perspex panel which does make it harder to see the frescoes or take pictures!

The frescoes show the nasty end the sinners get landed with in the Final Judgment. Find the temple where God is enthroned and surrounded by a hierarchy of the good on three levels, filled with angels and saints. The fourth level is a lurid depiction of hell, the seven deadly sins, and the fate which awaits the sinners. The frescoes were restored just before the end of the twentieth century.

Try to spot the small round device high in the dome at the foot of one of the windows. That is a gnomon and it is placed precisely so that the sun shines through it on the summer solstice at noon. It traces a pattern across the floor of the cathedral. It is a grand spectacle and the crowds gather:

https://www.youtube.com/watch?v=sSJwohj-v_w

Also take time to look at the round stained glass windows created by Donatello, Ghiberti and others – they are in the drum of the dome.

The last section of the climb is back inside the dome wall, and up a very steep stairway to the outside balcony. Once you get there you will have excellent views of all over Florence – and to the Campanile which is just next door. When you have seen enough, return to the ground and make your way back to the front of the Cathedral.

The Campanile
Face the front of the Cathedral and walk around the right-hand side to approach the Campanile.

Giotto is seen as one of the fathers of the Renaissance, leaving the older Byzantine methods of art and architecture behind. His campanile, as you can see, is beautifully sculpted and covered in marble decoration. When Giotto was asked by the Wool Guild to work on the campanile he was already 67. He died in 1337 at 71, long before it was completed – in fact the builders had only reached the first floor. However his design was followed by Pisano – at least until the builders reached the second floor. At that point Pisano decided to open the tower up more and we see the stunning result.

Take a walk around the outside of the Campanile and have a look at the hexagonal panels on the ground floor which were sculpted by Pisano himself. They show key moments in the history of man, starting of course with The Book of Genesis.

On the next level the panels show allegorical figures, like the planets, and "Faith Hope and Charity", but they are a little more difficult to see clearly.

It is thought that at one point the Campanile was joined to the Cathedral by a footbridge, but that disappeared centuries ago and since then it's been a standalone building.

The campanile also stars in a video game of all things - climbing the tower is one of the aims of the game Assassins Creed II – but they do it the hard way, from the outside! You of course can do it the easy way. The entrance and queue is on the other side of the tower from the Baptistery. From the top of the bell-tower you will get a wonderful view of the Tuscan hills, so tackle those 414 steps, but don't worry, there are some platforms where you can stop to catch a breather.

When you have had enough, exit and head for the Baptistery which is just opposite the Cathedral main door. At the time of writing, the entrance is opposite the ticket office you visited earlier – but the Baptistery exterior is being renovated so it may move.

Baptistery Interior

Before you go inside the baptistery, try to imagine eleventh century Florence. The dark ages are just fading away but the explosion of art of the Renaissance hasn't begun yet.

Step inside and imagine how the baptistery must have seemed to families arriving to have their new-born baptised - it glows and gleams and must have seemed enchanted. All Catholic Florentines were baptized here right up until the nineteenth century.

The altar and the walls are in beautifully decorated and intricate marble.

Font from Santa Reparata

The font from Santa Reparata was put in the Baptistery in the twelfth century but was later removed by order of the Grand Duke and replaced with the font you see against the wall today. But you can still see the outline of the old base in the middle of the floor – it's roped off.

Strozzo Strozzi

Have a look at the rather faded marble inlay covered in the signs of the zodiac - it's very old so you need to look closely to see the details. It was added to the Baptistery by Strozzo Strozzi, an astrologer who was also a captain in the army and who was chosen to lead the Florentine army in its battle with Fiesole, the nearby hilltop town – Florence won! The inscription is difficult to read, it's in Latin:

> EN GIRO TORTE SOL CICLOS ET ROTOR IGNE

Which translates as:

> With my fire I, the sun, make the circles move around and I move around too.

If you are very observant you might notice that the Latin can be read backwards as well. An opening in the dome which is now sealed let the sun hit the signs of the Zodiac. You can see the engraved blazing sun at the centre which was hit at the summer solstice, June 24, which happens to be the feast day of St John, the patron saint of Florence. Unfortunately the Baptistery floor was rearranged and the marbles re-laid in the thirteenth century, so even if the opening was re-opened it would no longer work.

Antipope John XXIII

The huge tomb against the wall is that of Antipope John XXIII. It's an odd title and it's not because he was against the Papacy – quite the opposite. An antipope is one who is not recognised by the church in Rome, but who has a good claim and support for the title.

The Catholic Church split three ways in the early fifteenth century and each sect elected its own Pope. It was called The Western Schism. Each Pope was supported by various parts of Europe, and Florence supported Pope John XXIII. This might have had something to with his decision to make the Medici Bank the papacy bank – making the Medici family mega-rich.

The various Popes busied themselves excommunicating each other and those parts of Europe which didn't support them. The church finally realigned and the popes all resigned or were sacked to let a new one be selected. Pope John XXIII eventually returned to Florence as Cardinal.

When he died, the Medici family commissioned this tomb by Donatello who was also a supporter of Pope John XXIII. The new Pope in Rome objected furiously to this very ornate and papal-like sarcophagus to no avail. John XXIII was the last pope to be buried outside of Rome. In fact Rome did not recognize him as Pope, which is why a Pope last century was also called Pope John XXIII..

The Dome

Sit down and take it all in.

The dome is covered in mosaics telling the story of The Final Judgment. Jesus sits centre-stage deciding the fate of all mankind. On the left hand side of Jesus, an Angel blows a trumpet heralding the good into heaven, whereas the wicked are met by demons and we see gory scenes of people meeting a truly nasty fate, being stoned, roasted, or perhaps devoured. Satan himself is there gorging on one of the unfortunate.

There is also an upper level which you can see and which is reached by a staircase inside the wall, but it's not open to the public.

When you return outside it's probably time to tackle the cathedral which opens last.

The Cathedral Interior

Again standing in front of the cathedral you can see the queue for the Cathedral's interior snaking down the left hand

24

side. Note, entrance to the Cathedral is still free so you don't need your receipt to get in. Of course that also means you can't skip the queue – and it is a long queue!

The queue moves along quite speedily, mainly because there is not really much to see inside. The Cathedral is impressively huge, but to be honest it's quite bare inside and compared with the interiors of other Tuscan cathedrals it's a bit of a let-down. What makes it worse is the crowd control measures the Cathedral uses – you will be funnelled down one side of the Cathedral, then diagonally across the middle to exit the other side. I expect no-one spends any more than fifteen minutes inside, so if you thought you would find a pew to take in the view – think again.

Once inside, turn around to have a look at the church clock.

The clock

The huge one-handed clock sits above the main door and it is still working. It runs in Italian time - all other clocks in the world now run on French time. It's really more akin to a sundial in that it is made to follow the movement of the sun - this was quite a common system until the fifteenth century when everyone switched to the simpler French system.

It has sections for the 24 hours of the day, with number 24 at the bottom rather than the top. The 24th hour actually indicates sunset, which of course is a moving target through the year. So the clock is re-set each week to ensure that the last hour of daylight lands on the 24th hour.

The clock was modified to have a 12 hour face at one time, and the original wasn't discovered until 1973 during a restoration.

The Memorials

The Cathedral was funded by the state of Florence and not the church. This had the result that the state could dictate to

25

some extent on what was put inside it. That is why you will find statues and memorials to an odd collection of individuals.

On your left as you walk down the side of the cathedral are several busts. The second one from the door is Cambio who actually designed the cathedral.

Continue and a little further down you will see the huge memorials to two soldiers.

One is to Niccolò da Tolentino who is shown in rather a natty hat! The next is John Hawkwood from England. He was a very successful mercenary who actually fought against Florence at one point, but then came over to their side and was paid well for his efforts! He saved the city from invasion by the Viscount of Milan who was expanding his empire rapidly and sweeping southwards. When he died he was seen as a hero, hence this memorial.

Dante

Find the painting called "Dante and the Divine Comedy". Dante was Italy's most famous poet and he came from Florence. Here you see Dante in sixteenth century Florence gazing at Hell, the Mountain of Purgatory, and Paradise with Adam and Eve, all scenes from his most famous piece of work The Divine Comedy.

This is a bit of an odd painting as Dante died in 1321 as an exile. However over the centuries he came back into favour and got this memorial in the cathedral. You will read more about him later as you stroll through Florence as he pops up in various places.

When you reach the end of the allowed route on this left hand side of the cathedral, you might be interested to know that right at the back of the cathedral is the silver shrine of St Zenobious whose column you saw outside – but of course you can't see it!

At this point you will get the best view of the dome, just as the route swings across the Cathedral to the other side.

The Floor

The Wool Merchants, who were in charge of the Cathedral's construction, organised themselves into a committee called the Opera del Duomo or OPA for short – it was their logo. You can see an example of the OPA symbol on the door. It's also on the Cathedral floor.

You will see their guild symbol in various places, including some stained glass windows. Appropriately for wool merchants, their symbol is a lamb with a cross.

Near the exit you will find the stairs to take you down to the crypt – you need your receipt for this visit. Once downstairs you are at least free to roam about, staying on the walkways.

The Crypt

This is where you can see the remains of the old cathedral, Santa Reparata. The nicest evidence is probably pieces of the original mosaic floor.

Santa Reparata church was much smaller than the Cathedral. If you stand at the main door of the Cathedral, the old church would only have stretched to about quarter of the Cathedral's length.

Reparata was a martyr from the third century who was arrested for the crime of being Christian. Her captors tried to burn her alive, but God sent a rainstorm and saved her. She was then made to drink boiling pitch and she survived that too, although there is no mention of how! She was then beheaded and that finally finished her off. Her spirit soared into the air as a dove. Her body was put on a boat and blown by angels into the Bay of Angels in Nice in southern France.

Brunellsechi

Find the tomb of Filippo Brunelleschi, the architect of the dome – it was only rediscovered in the 1970s. On his tomb is an inscription which translates as:

> "Both the magnificent dome of this famous church and many other devices invented by Filippo the architect, bear witness to his superb skill. Therefore, in tribute to his exceptional talents, a grateful country that will always remember buries him here in the soil below"

Giotto

Giotto designed the campanile. When he died he was buried in Santa Reparata, but no-one knew where. During an excavation of Santa Reparata a grave was found which forensicologists believe was probably an artist.

The first clue is that the bones when analysed had a high level of arsenic and lead, deemed to be from paint. Secondly, the man's body was only four feet tall and he died about the age of 70. Thirdly, the skeleton proved that he spent a lot of time with his head tilted backwards! Fourth, his front teeth were worn away which could be caused by holding a brush with his teeth. Finally any image of Giotto depicted him as a very small man. It may be total nonsense, but the authorities had enough doubt to bury the remains near the grave of Brunelleschi.

Giotto and Brunelleschi busts

Go back upstairs and you will find you are at the Cathedral exit – that didn't take long did it? Before you exit glance down the wall towards the main door and you will see several busts on the wall. One is Giotto who designed the Campanile and one is Brunelleschi who devised the Dome.

When you have had enough return outside

There are still some items to be seen on this square. Stand between the Cathedral and the Baptistery and face the Baptistery. Turn left to find the colonnaded Loggia del Bigallo.

Loggia del Bigallo

This pretty place has a complicated history. It was built in the fourteenth century for the brothers of the Compagnia della Misericordia, who later joined forces with the neighbouring Compagnia del Bigallo. The two companies split apart again in the sixteenth century, leaving the Compagnia del Bigallo in sole residence – hence the building's current name.

The companies were founded to help those in dire need. The Compagnia della Misericordia took on the horrendous task of disposing of corpses – including plague victims. They are still in existence and you might see an ambulance parked opposite where their current offices lie – although they no longer wear long black hooded robes!

The Compagnia del Bigallo had a more cheerful task, they rescued lost or abandoned children. This little loggia was where the children were housed by the brothers in the hope that a relative would claim them.

The Loggia is now used as a tourist office, but you can enquire about the time of the next tour of the Loggia itself.

29

They don't get many people asking about it, as it's very small and not well known. You will probably be given a time later in the day – so if you think you can make it, put your name down and return later. If you do get inside you will get a handy little guide book.

There are numerous frescoes. The most interesting is The Madonna della Misericordia, which shows the oldest known depiction of Florence - from the fourteenth century. If you look at the Virgin's feet you can spot the Baptistery and the Cathedral during its construction. The old cathedral of Santa Reparata is still there and you can see its roof and bell-towers.

Another fresco shows the brothers placing orphans with new parents, when all hope of their being claimed had gone.

Back outside have a look at the fresco above the Loggia's columns and facing the Baptistery. It's a bit faded but you can just make out a black horse racing past and a man holding his arms out. It relates to an old legend. In the thirteenth century Saint Peter the Martyr was preaching against heretics in Piazza della Repubblica – which you will visit on walk 2. A black horse went wild and was thrashing at the crowd. The saint declared it was the devil and held his arms out to turn himself into the shape of a cross. The horse turned and raced away down Via Strozzi where it disappeared. You will see another reminder of this story on walk 2.

With both the loggia and the Baptistery behind you, walk straight ahead to walk along the south side of the cathedral. On your right you will see the Cannon's Palace

Cannon's Palace

This building is interesting because of the two statues at its front. The man looking up at the dome is Brunelleschi– gazing in pride at his wonderful construction. The other one is Cambio who was responsible for the cathedral's original design.

Brunelleschi was not only an architect and sculptor, but also fancied himself as a shipbuilder. He built a huge ship called Il Badalone to move marble up and down the Arno. Brunelleschi also took out one of the world's first patents for his ship, and if any ship was constructed using the same design it would be burned. However just like the Titanic, Il Badalone sank on its maiden voyage. No-one knows why but there was a lot of animosity regarding that patent.

A curiosity here is a stone embedded into the front of the building which is inscribed with "Sasso di Dante". This is reputedly where Dante sat to gaze at the cathedral as it was being constructed and dreamt up The Divine Comedy. However there is a more likely stone around the corner in Piazza delle Pallottole – so you could pop round to compare them. Whichever is the real stone, many famous posteriors have copied Dante. Charles Dickens even mentions it in Little Dorrit as he describes Dante:

He used to put leaves round his head, and sit on a stool for some unaccountable purpose, outside the cathedral at Florence.

Wordsworth wrote the following in his poem Memorials of a tour in Italy:

> I stood and gazed upon a marble stone,
>
> The Laurelled Dante's favourite seat – a throne

The Dome's Ball

Another little curiosity is a large white circle marble stone, which you will find on the ground a little further along the Cathedral from the Cannon's Palace. During a lightning storm in 1601 the dome was hit and the huge ball which sits at the top of the cathedral crashed to the ground, and this plaque marks the spot where it hit the ground. Amazingly no-one was hurt – it weighed eighteen hundred kilos and the crash was heard all over town.

The ball was repaired and put back up again. Nowadays the Cathedral is protected against lightning by a conductor so you should be safe enough.

Walk past the Cathedral to reach the Museo del Duomo.

Museo del Duomo

This is another museum full of treasures and how long you spend will depend on how much time you have and how much you want to see the rest of Florence. If you go in, do try to see the following:

Mary Magdalen

Mary Magdalen of course was the sinful woman who became a follower of Christ, and is portrayed in many famous paintings. She is usually shown either at the cross, or washing and drying Christ's feet.

After the crucifixion she became a hermit, lived in a cave, and devoted herself to prayer. Donatello carved her as she might have been seen many years later, looking gaunt and sad. She appears to be wearing rags, but it is actually her own hair wrapped around her body.

This statue used to stand in the Baptistery, but again was moved for its own safety.

Beheading of John the Baptist

This group of statues has been taken from above the South door of the Baptistery, and so far has not been replaced with any copy – which is very disappointing. So here are the originals. The figure on the left is Salome who is waiting to receive the head of John the Baptist. You can see she is braced and trying to protect herself from the spray of blood.

The Gates of Paradise

These are the originals which have been out of sight for 27 years as they were restored. They now glow the way they did centuries ago.

Michelangelo's Pieta

Michelangelo produced this work of art near the end of his life, and planned that it be placed on his own tomb. However he was dissatisfied with it and tried to destroy it in frustration, but it was later restored by one of his students.

Altar of St John

This silver masterpiece was originally for the Baptistery and shows the life of John the Baptist. It contains a whacking 250 kilograms of silver

Canto di Bischeri

Once you are back outside, take a look at the corner of Via dell'Oriuolo and you will see a plaque inscribed with Canto di Bischeri. This at one time was the corner of the Palazzo Bischeri, the home of another of Florence's wealthy families. Bischeri today means

> "Someone who doesn't take the smartest path".

Why? Because when the Cathedral was planned it needed a lot of space, and anyone who had a building on the proposed site were generously compensated to give up their property. The Bischeri family decided to say no, perhaps hoping for a better offer. The Cathedral works ground to a halt, until one night the palazzo went up in flames. Coincidence I am sure.

To leave the square, return to The Cannon's Palace and face Bruneschelli. Take the little street to your left, Via del Studio.

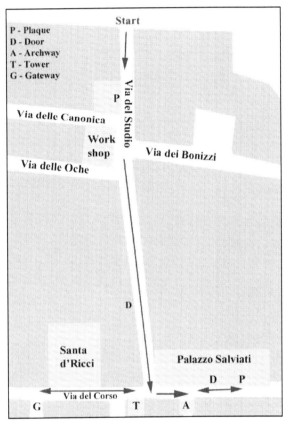

The Devil's Whirlwind

There is an old legend about this street. You might notice a breeze as you walk down it, and if it's a windy day you will find a howling gale. The locals call this wind the Devil's whirlwind. The story tells of a priest who escaped from the devil by running into the Cathedral by one door and out by another. The devil became very angry, so he started to blow and created the whirlwind.

As you walk downhill you will pass an old tower on the right. This was the birthplace of one of Florence's local saints, Saint Antoninus of Florence, commemorated by a bust of the saint above the door and a plaque

Just a little further on is a single story building, which houses the Cathedral's stonemason's workshop. You can peep in the windows to see what is being worked on. It has an interesting engraving outside showing the men at work – even if they do look like they are about to commit murder!

Continue along Via del Studio and you will reach an old wooden door on your right. It was the entrance to the original University of Florence called the Studium Generale which opened in 1348. There is a badly damaged Medici coat of arms above the door, and above that a sculpture engraved with the OPA symbol, which you saw earlier in the Cathedral.

Florence's university never really took off and limped along without enough money or students. It was transferred to Pisa in the fifteenth century by order of Lorenzo the Magnificent. It seems an odd thing to do, but apparently Lorenzo saw it as a diplomatic move to improve relations with Pisa. Pisa University is now ranked as the best in Italy.

You have now reached a T junction with Via del Corso. Turn right and about 50 feet along on your right is Santa de'Ricci church. Pop in to see the Madonna dei Ricci.

Madonna di Ricci

At one time there was an image of the Virgin Mary on a nearby piazza. One night at the start of the fifteenth century, it was pelted with horse manure by a drunken gambler who had lost his money. He was spotted, arrested, and hung from the windows of the nearby Bargello. This church was built both to house the Madonna's image, and to acknowledge what was seen as a fitting punishment. Inside the church you will find the image above the main altar - it is known as the Madonna di Ricci. You can see the full story of the incident depicted in a side room.

The church's story does not end there.

In 1978 a crucifix in the church was attacked with a hammer, and photographs were taken of the enraged face of Christ. The crucifix is now in a glass case next to the Madonna di Ricci and Christ's face has returned to a more normal expression. Have a look at the photographs and make your own mind up! The attacker was never found.

Leave the church and turn right. Just a few yards further along you will reach an old gateway which is usually shut.

Donati Cerchi Gateway

You have already read about the feuds between the Guelphs and Ghibellines which the Guelphs eventually won. Two of the richest Guelph families, the Donati and the Cerchi, started another feud which split Florence once more, this time into the White Guelphs and the Black Guelphs. The Donati and the Cerchi were neighbours and the feud erupted into battles and attacks. The city council stepped in and put gates on both sides of this passageway to try to keep the two families apart.

Back track now past the Santa de'Ricci church. Just before you reach Via dello Studio again you will see another ancient tower on your right. That is the Torre dei Donati, and belonged to one of feuding families you have just read about.

Torre dei Donati

Dante had a very low opinion of the families involved in the White/Black Guelph split, and blamed them for the turmoil and lawlessness of Florence. If you look up you will see a plaque inscribed with the words he gave to Forese Donati in The Devine Comedy. Forese states that his brother is the main cause of all Florence's troubles.

Once you reach Via dello Studio you will find an archway on your right into Via Margherita. Before you go through the archway, have a look at the building opposite it, the Palazzo Portinari Salviati.

Palazzo Portinari Salviati

This is the magnificent family home of Dante's love Beatrice Portinari, which is now a bank. It's a sad love story because although Dante worshipped her from the moment he first saw her in this palace, he never approached her. Beatrice never knew of his love, married another, and died at just twenty-four. Dante placed her in the Divine Comedy as one of his guides through the afterlife.

Walk a little beyond the main entrance of the Palazzo and you will see a stone on the façade with Dante's verses about his one true love.

> A lady appeared to me
>
> beneath a green mantle
>
> dressed in the colour of a living flame

Backtrack and go through the archway.

Santa Margherita de Cerchi

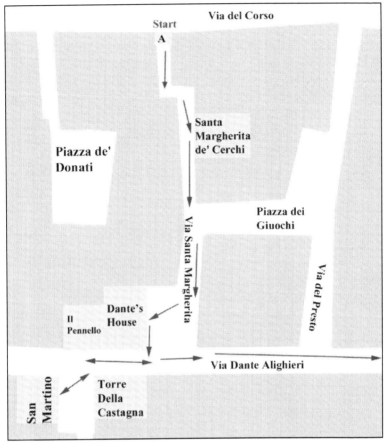

The archway is part of Santa Margherita de' Cerchi which is on your left, and is where Dante married the woman he had long been betrothed to, who happened to be Beatrice's cousin, Gemma Donati.

This church was the Donati parish church and does contain tombs of some of the Portinari family, although probably not Beatrice who would have been buried in her husband's family church. The church lets visitors leave notes to Beatrice asking for help in their love lives – if you feel the need you can leave one in the basket next to her supposed shrine – it's on your left hand side.

Continue down this little street which opens out to a little square. You will find Dante's House on your right.

Dante's House

Dante certainly lived in this area, but not in this actual house, but it's atmospheric and good for a snap. Inside there are many rooms, but only two of them are about Dante specifically. However the other rooms do provide a lot of interesting pictures and information on medieval Florence. If you have the Firenze card it's worth a look – and it does have a nice little gift shop downstairs.

Dante's most famous work is The Divine Comedy, a very long poem (over 14,000 lines!!) which is regarded as one of Italy's greatest works. It describes the afterlife as seen in mediaeval times: in it Dante visits Hell, Purgatory, and Paradise.

You might have heard or read of Dante's "Inferno" or the "Circles of Hell" and wondered what it all meant. Well, Dante saw the afterlife as containing two structures. There were 9 descending circles of hell with the Devil at the bottom in one, and 9 rising rings on the mountain of purgatory topped by Heaven in the other. It gets a lot more complicated than that depending on just why you were cast into hell or purgatory.

Dante had political problems in his life. He was a Guelph, which meant he supported the Pope, as opposed to the Ghibellines who supported the monarchy. Most of Tuscany was split along these lines and it provided a reason for endless battles over the centuries. The Guelphs later split even further into white and black Guelphs. Dante was a white Guelph and unfortunately they were exiled from Florence in 1302. In fact, if he had returned to Florence he would have been burned at the stake. That sentence was only rescinded by Florence in 2008! He left his home city and retaliated by dropping his enemies into the various circles of hell in The Divine Comedy.

Dante is so revered in Italy that they put his image on one of their coins, a bit like Shakespeare on the British twenty pound note. Also Asteroid 2999 Dante was named after Italy's most famous poet.

If you feel the need for some light reading you could always buy a copy of the Divine Comedy in the gift shop.

When you leave the museum turn right to reach Via Dante Alighieri. Take a short detour right to reach Piazza San Martino.

San Martino

The door at the corner of the church of Saint Martin is the entrance to a very old and unusual charity which is still in existence. It started in 1441 and its purpose was to help the well-off families of Florence who went bankrupt, but were too proud to ask for help.

Even today the charity will gauge and help families who are in difficulty. To qualify for help the applicant must have been in Florence for ten years, must be of good character, and must have no other source of income. There are twelve officers, two for each of the districts of Florence. If the applicant is successful, one of the officers will visit the applicant's home to hand over the cash personally. This means the applicant doesn't have to be embarrassed by turning up at the office.

If the charity runs out of money, the officers light a candle in the window on one side of the door to let the people know. Donations are posted into the cross shaped hole you see on the other side of the door. A local saying came into being, "reduced to a flicker", meaning in dire financial straits.

Torre Della Castagna

Opposite the church is the Torre Della castagna, another very old tower. Florence's Town Hall, the Palazzo Vecchio which you will see on Walk 2, was built at the very end of the thirteenth century. Until then town council meetings were held in the Torre Della Castagna.

Castagna means chestnut, and the tower gets its odd name because the council would vote by placing a chestnut in the Yes or No bag. Interestingly the local word for boiled chestnut is ballotta, and it's thought to be where the word ballot comes from.

Il Pennello

Il Pennello means The Brush, and it is a little restaurant facing onto Piazza San Martino. It used to be a tavern which was owned by the painter Albertinelli, and was visited by many artists including Michelangelo and Cellini. It was turned into a restaurant at the end of the nineteenth century, and its original owner is commemorated by the terracotta plaque outside which depicts Albertinelli.

Backtrack along Via Dante Alighieri, and pass Via del Presto on your left.

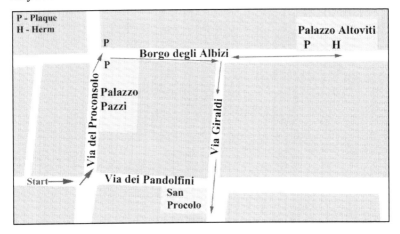

When you reach the next junction turn left into Via del Proconsolo. As you approach the next junction you will see the distinctive Palazzo Pazzi on your right.

Palazzo Pazzi

This is thought to be one of the most beautiful palaces in Florence and was constructed by the Pazzi family. They were enemies of the all-powerful Medici family and they tried to take over Florence via the Pazzi Conspiracy - a plot which resulted in the murder of Guiliano de Medici and the wounding of his brother Lorenzo Medici in the Cathedral. Lorenzo survived by running into the sacristy of the Cathedral and hiding there until his own guards arrived to rescue him.

Francesco de' Pazzi ran back to this building bleeding after the murder. The leaders of the plot were soon caught and hung in a gruesome fashion. The survivors of the family were exiled and their palace was confiscated – they were only allowed back into Florence twenty years later.

Sadly you can't actually get into the courtyard, but if you could you would see columns topped with sculpted dolphins, one of the Pazzi family's symbols. There are also vases of sacred fire inscribed on the columns –those commemorate Pazzino de' Pazzi who was a hero of the first crusade. He was one of the first over the walls of Jerusalem and raised the Christian flag. He also brought back three pieces of flint from Jerusalem, which are still used today in a special ceremony, The Explosion of the Cart.

At Easter a priest creates a spark with the Pazzi flint-stones and lights a candle in the Church of Santi Apostoli. The candle is used to light some torches which are then carried to the Cathedral in a grand procession. They are then used to ignite a fuse which runs down a wire from the Cathedral altar to a cart full of fireworks placed between the Cathedral and the Baptistery. The Campanile's bells ring out throughout the entire procedure. If the fireworks are successful, it foretells a lucky year for Florence. If you would like to see it, you can find a video on https://www.youtube.com/

Continue to the corner with Borgo degli Albizi and on the wall you will see a plaque bearing the inscription Canto dei Pazzi – Corner of the Pazzi. After the Pazzi conspiracy, the Medici family introduced a law forbidding anyone to use that name ever again, although they left the Pazzi coat of arms which you can see above you on the right – again with the dolphins.

Palazzo Altoviti

Now turn right to walk along narrow Borgo degli Albizi, passing Via Giraldi on the right. On your left further up the street you will find the very distinctive Palazzo Altoviti, which was the family home of one of Florence's wealthy families.

It is decorated with busts of famous Florentines, including Vespucci and Dante. The busts have a nickname, "Visacci", or "ugly faces". The technical term for this style of bust is "herm", which means a bust on top of a slim tapered block.

Spot the plaque under the first window you reach. It tells the story (in Latin) of one of the miracles of Saint Zenobius – the same saint who watches over his column in the Piazza di Duomo. The Bishop came across a woman carrying the body of her dead son and weeping profusely. The bishop touched the boy and he came back to life on this spot.

Back track and at the first junction you reach, turn left down Via Giraldi. Walk down this street to the junction with Via dei Pandolfini. At the corner of the junction you will see San Procolo.

San Procolo

This is a very old church first built in the thirteenth century, and was home to various religious bodies over the centuries. In the eighteenth century it was given to the brothers of Sant'Antonio Abate dei Macellai - a flagellant brotherhood who whipped themselves in an attempt to appease God. The church did have several paintings by Fra Lippi but they are now safely stashed in the Academia and the Uffizi.

The church has survived various disasters, the last in 2005 when the roof collapsed and had to be rebuilt. Various neighbouring businesses had offered to buy it, including a hotel and The Bargello museum which is nearby. So when you pass this way it may be open for some sort of business again.

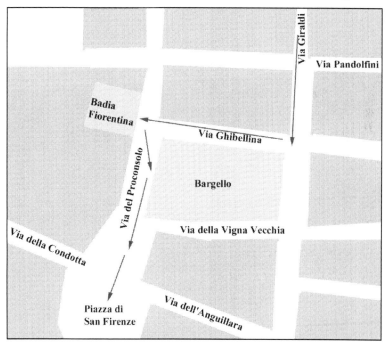

Continue down Via Giraldi then turn right into Via Ghibellina. You can see the very pretty Badia Fiorentina bell tower. You can see that the tower is pointed rather than square at the top. When you tackle walk 5 to see Florence from a hilltop, you will be able to pick this tower out easily. Walk towards the tower and onto Via del Proconsolo.

Badia Fiorentina

The Badia Fiorentina, the city's oldest monastery, is in front of you. It was built in the tenth century against the city wall as it stood at that time. Its main benefactor at that time was Ugo the Marquis of Tuscany, although it was his mother who actually founded the monastery in the tenth century.

Why was Ugo so generous? Because one day he got lost in the forest whilst hunting, and had a vision of devils torturing and tormenting lost souls. Ugo basically took fright and started donating his money to religious bodies, including this monastery. Ugo is buried in the church and the abbey still says a mass for him every year on December 21st which is Saint Thomas's day. You will find a Dante plaque just to the right of the door stating this fact. Dante calls Ugo the "Great Baron" and places him in Paradise, so he clearly thought Ugo was one of the good guys.

The abbey was modified and improved over the centuries – the industrious monks acquired a lot of the surrounding buildings and created a money-making book production industry. However the monks failed to pay their taxes in 1307 and as a punishment the original lovely belfry was chopped down! It was replaced by the current bell-tower in the fourteenth century. It's Romanesque (square and clunky) at the base and Gothic (lacy stonework) at the top. The bell in the pretty tower was used to mark the start and the end of the working day – but it hasn't rung for a very long time.

Once you enter from the street door you will find the entrance to the church itself through another door on your left. This church is surprisingly unvisited by tourists, perhaps because the nuns and monks want to keep it that way. The community of monks and nuns sing Vespers every day around 6:00pm. You might want to plan a discrete visit then as the singing is worth hearing.

Look up to see its beautiful ornate ceiling. The church holds one masterpiece, "The Virgin Appearing to St Barnard" by Filippino Lippi who was a pupil of Botticelli. It is one of his most admired works. It shows the Virgin helping Saint Barnard to fight against evil, spot the devils in chains lurking beneath the rocks just behind the saint. It's in the gloomy left hand corner as you enter the church. You can pop a coin in to light it up to get a better look.

Ugo's tomb is also worth a glance. Approach the altar and look to your left when you reach the transept. The tomb is made of marble and porphyry and apparently people have had visions while visiting it – so you might be lucky!

Pop into the pretty little Cloister of the Oranges which is on two floors - if it is open. The entrance is at the back of the church on the right hand side – but it only opens on Monday afternoons. The orange trees are long gone but it's full of colour from its frescoes.

Exit the church and you will find the Museo del Bargello just opposite.

Museo del Bargello

Nowadays this building is a must-see museum, but as you walk through the colonnaded courtyard, consider that at one time it was where criminals met their end. The Podesta, the city magistrate, sat here and dispensed justice, and when required the sentences were carried out in this courtyard. If you look round the courtyard you will see the coats of arms of the various Podestas.

Leonardo Da Vinci sketched the hanging of Bernardo Bandini who was one of the Pazzi conspirators. He was hung from the one of the windows of the Bargello

48

The Michelangelo room

The Michelangelo room is just next to the door you entered the courtyard by.

Standing near the entrance is Michelangelo's Baachus looking very drunk and clutching his goblet of wine. This statue is actually often criticised as not being up to Michelangelo's usual high standard. When Shelly visited Florence and saw the statue he said

> "It looks drunken, brutal, and narrow-minded, and has an expression of dissoluteness the most revolting."

But who knows, perhaps that is exactly what Michelangelo intended.

Also in this room is a bust of Brutus – who of course is famous for the assassination of the tyrannical Julius Caesar. Michelangelo is believed to have been unhappy with the Medici family's rule of Tuscany, so perhaps sculpting Brutus was a muted protest. Michelangelo copied the features of Brutus from an ancient engraving so it might be a good likeness.

Go back outside to the courtyard, cross it, and go up the stairs to the first floor. Find the Donatello room.

The Donatello room

This beautiful room with its high arches and stained glass windows was where the council met but now holds Donatello's masterpieces. Dante was sentenced to exile from Florence in this room.

Donatello's Davids

Compare Donatello's two Davids. The slender young David in marble was made in Donatello's youth, and the bronze was thirty years later. The bronze David was the first freestanding naked statue to be sculpted since classical times – naked apart from his hat and boots of course!

Everyone knows the story of David from the book of Samuel. The Philistines and Israelites were at war. The Philistines sent their mighty warrior Goliath to decide the battle in a man-to-man battle. The Israeli soldiers took one look at Goliath and backed off. So David, who was only a shepherd boy, stood up, refused any armour, and brought Goliath down with one shot from his sling. This statue has Goliath's head lying at David's feet.

Many people are puzzled by the very feminine appeal of David, from his dinky hat, to his rather female figure. It's been suggested that Donatello was homosexual, which might have something to do with this rendition of David.

50

Baptistery Doors Competition

Go to the back wall of the Donatello room. You can compare the two winning entrants of the Baptistery doors commission you see in front of you. The contest's remit was to illustrate the Sacrifice of Isaac - that's the Old Testament story where Abraham was commanded by God to sacrifice his son Isaac. The judges decided both these panels were so good that both artists should work on the Baptistery doors; however Brunelleschi's pride was hurt at not being first choice, and left for Rome in a bit of a huff leaving Ghiberti to produced his masterpieces.

Experts have pointed out that the Ghiberti panel has a mountain background, whereas Brunelleschi's panel doesn't really have any background at all. Which one do you prefer?

Saint George

The statue of Saint George is greatly admired. This is another well-known story. A dragon was terrorizing the town of Silene which was in Libya. The town sacrificed two sheep a day to placate the dragon, but the dragon demanded more, in other words it wanted people. Silene started a lottery of the town's youth and the poor victim was led out to the dragon, until the day the Princess's name came up. The princess was actually outside awaiting her fate when Saint George rode up. He heard her sad tale and promptly slew the dragon with his lance. In gratitude Silene converted to Christianity on the spot.

Don't miss looking at the panel below Saint George. It shows Donatello's revolutionary technique of perspective – the loggia arcades on the right hand side of the panel decrease in size as they recede – that was an entirely new concept.

The statue used to stand on the outside of the Orsanmichele church, along with a whole army of saints. You will see its original home on Walk 4.

Marzocco

This room is also the home of Donatello's Marzocco – the lion which is a famous symbol of Florence. This statue originally stood in the Piazza della Signoria as a replacement for the original Marzocco which had worn away to a lump of stone. Now of course Donatello's rendition is safely tucked away here in the Bargello and has itself been replaced. You will see its replacement on walk 2.

Marzocco was a powerful symbol for Florence and adorned Tuscany's first postage stamp in the mid nineteenth century. The lion holds the coat of arms of Florence with one paw, and when Florence went into battle, Marzocco was the battle cry. If you explore Tuscany, you will see Marzocco appear in various locations which fell under the rule of Florence.

Podesta Chapel

One last room to find is the Mary Magdalene chapel, originally the Podesta chapel. This is where criminals received the last rites before being dispatched in the courtyard.

The frescoes on the walls are by Giotto, and they were only discovered in the nineteenth century. They show Heaven and Hell which is appropriate given the chapels clientele. You also see a very old portrait of Dante – he is dressed in red and has been restored and stands out from the rest of the fresco.

When you exit the museum, turn left to reach Piazza di San Firenze

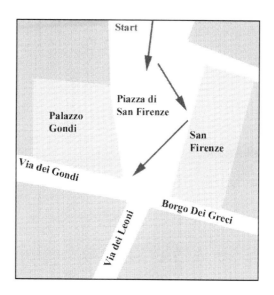

Piazza di San Firenze

The entrance to this square used to be full of parked motorbikes however it has recently been rescued and is now a pedestrian zone.

Walk through the square and you will find a very large church on your left at the top of some steps.

San Filippo Neri

It's thought that this site was originally a temple to the Egyptian god Isis. They did find a statue of a Roman Senator when the church was excavated – it was immediately whisked across the square to the courtyard of Palazzo Gondi.

The church complex originally consisted of a church on one side, an oratory on the other side, and a seminary in the middle. The church has always remained a church, and if it's open pop in to see its golden ceiling.

The rest of the building was until recently a law court. However the law has moved out and the building is now used for exhibitions – so you might find something of interest as you pass.

Opposite San Firenze is the Palazzo Gondi.

Palazzo Gondi

This is another of Florence's beautiful palaces. It was built over some dilapidated housing which is believed to be where Leonardo da Vinci lived while he was painting the Mona Lisa.

It has a beautiful courtyard where the Roman statue found across the square now stands. If you can get into the courtyard, spot an inscription above the doorway which marks it as the location of Leonardo Da Vinci's studio.

Before leaving the square make sure you look back to see the best view of the Badia Fiorentina bell tower

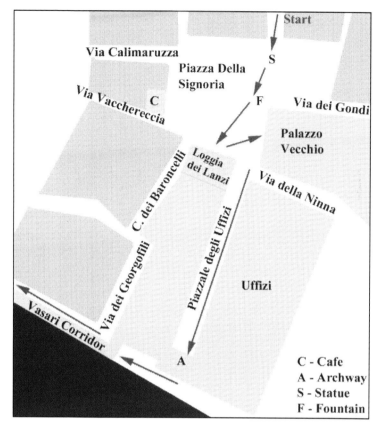

At the end of the square continue straight ahead into Via dei Leoni. Pass Via dei Gondi on your right and Via Vinegia on your left. When you reach the next crossroads you will find the Loggia del Granno

Loggia del Granno

Grain was stored in the upper floors and traded from the ground floor. Grain was a serious business as it was a staple food and supply had to be maintained. The Loggia was policed by grain officers and anyone found selling poor quality grain would be imprisoned or banished.

This loggia was built when the old grain store morphed into a church after workers experienced a few visions – you will see it on walk 4. The loggia has a pretty fountain at the corner.

Continue straight ahead into Via dei Castellani and eventually you will reach the river Arno. Turn right for the best view of the Ponte Vecchio.

Ponte Vecchio

This is Italy's most famous bridge, apart possibly from the Rialto Bridge in Venice. It is medieval, crosses the Arno where it is narrowest, and one of only a handful of bridges in the world with shops across it. It is first mentioned in written history in 996 AD, but that version was wooden and swept away by the furious Arno during a flood. In fact the bridge has been swept away and rebuilt more than once.

The Nazis chose not to destroy the Ponte Vecchio when they retreated, which was not their usual style. Legend says that the commander thought it too beautiful to destroy.

When you actually reach the bridge on walk 2 you might be disappointed as it is now very touristy, so enjoy it from here in relative peace.

Museo Galileo

You will have just passed the Museo Galileo on your right, full of all things astronomical from all over the world. Telescopes and other gadgets were beautifully designed and cunningly disguised as everyday items – perhaps because the church did not totally approve of all this gazing at the stars. Find the telescope disguised as a makeup box for the ladies and another built into a gentleman's walking stick!! They are upstairs and in one of the last rooms you will visit.

Probably most interesting for real aficionados are the telescopes which Galileo used to spot the moons of Jupiter.

Those of us with a more morbid taste will gaze at his finger which seems to be making a rather rude gesture, perhaps to Rome for taking nearly 400 years to believe his theories. The museum seems to be gathering bits of Galileo as they have his thumb, index, and middle finger – almost a hand!! They were removed when his remains were transferred to a new burial ground.

If you are expecting or even contemplating having a baby, you should avoid part of the second floor. It has vivid and frankly upsetting depictions on everything which can go wrong with a pregnancy, and it's a mystery why it is in this museum.

Outside the museum you will see a column and an etching in the pavement which shows the midday meridian, so if it's near noon you can see the sun mark the spot.

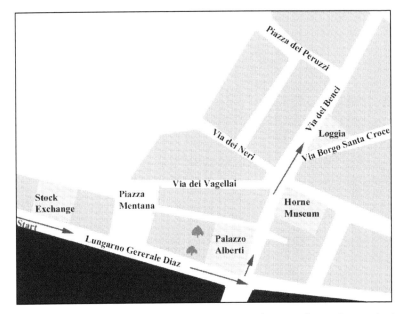

Turn left to walk along the river and past the colonnaded Stock Exchange.

The Arno used to be very important to the Tuscan towns and cities which lay on it, as it was the region's main highway. Leonardo da Vinci and Machiavelli came up with a devious plan to bankrupt Florence's one-time enemy Pisa, which lay downriver on the coast. They drew up plans to divert the Arno to leave Pisa high and dry – which for a port would have been financially disastrous.

Ditches were dug, but they weren't dug deep enough and the Arno stayed resolutely on its present day course. It's amusing to think that The Arno finally did what Da Vinci and Machiavelli were attempting. It brought down so much silt over the centuries that the delta was silted up, and Pisa now lies kilometres from the coast. Of course that took centuries to happen, so Pisa was able to adapt.

The river flows down from the Apennines and can turn into a raging torrent in an amazingly short time. It has flooded Florence more than once, but the worst occasion was in 1966 when Florence was under an overwhelming deluge. Lives were lost, and many works of art were ruined and are still languishing out of sight – waiting for a restoration of some sort.

You will reach the next bridge, Ponte alle Grazie. The last building on your left as you approach it is the Palazzo Alberti

Palazzo Alberti

This palazzo was the home of the extensive Alberti family – another of Florence's great families. Prior to the rise of the Medici family, the Alberti family were themselves at one time the key family in Florence. However they suffered the consequences of the Guelph-Ghibelline battles.

Continue to the bridge then turn left into Via dei Benci and walk to the next junction. On your right is the Horne museum which contains what was the private collection of Herbert Horne. He donated it to Florence in his will, and it contains a collection of Florentine art, furniture, ornamental and household objects, but you might be museumed out by now, and you still have one "must see" to tackle on this walk. So unless there is something in the museum you really want to see, continue straight ahead on Via dei Benci.

Loggia Degli Alberti

Notice the tower on your right with a colonnaded entrance which is a restaurant now. This is all that remains of an original huge palazzo which also belonged to the Alberti family. It stretched from this corner all the way to the next bridge and up to Sante Croce – it was huge. If you look at the top of the columns you can see the family coat of arms – two crossed chains. The palazzo was destroyed except for this one surviving tower in one of the furious battles between the Ghibellines and Guelphs.

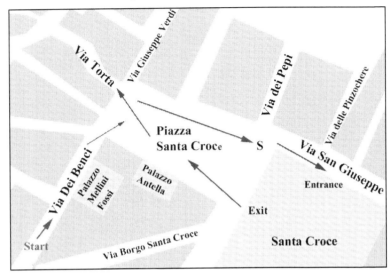

Continue along Via dei Benci. You will pass the front of another palace on your right, the Palazzo Mellini-Fossi.

Palazzo Mellini-Fossi

This palace was also owned by the Albertis. You can spot it by the frescoes which run along the facade. They were hidden under a layer of dirt for centuries, until Hitler arrived in Florence in 1938 – Florence was tidied up for the occasion, and the worst of the grime was removed. It was fully restored only in 1994. If you know your Greek legends you can try to spot Diana, Persus, Medusa and Andomeda.

Just a little further on the road will open out onto Piazza Santa Croce.

Piazza Santa Croce

This square has always been used for large civic events from medieval times, from May Day festivities, to carnival, and even jousting.

Calcio Storico

Every year in June, a football tournament takes place on this square, with everyone in period costume. It's actually an old tradition from the fifteenth century and was played by young men of the wealthy families.

Look to the right to the frescoed Palazzo Antella which has a bust of Cosmino II above the door. There is a handy plaque between two windows on the ground floor which is used as the halfway line of the football pitch.

It was and still is a violent game, more like rugby with fists than soccer. These days there are four teams from the four quarters of old Florence:

- Santa Croce - Blues
- Santa Maria Novella - Reds
- Santo Spirito - Whites
- San Giovanni – Greens

There are 27 in a team. The rules allow the players to head-butt, punch, elbow, and choke the other side. They do rule out kicks to the head, and only two players can try to annihilate each other at once – on penalty of being sent off. The winning side is presented with a cow! You can have a look on Youtube

Basilica di Santa Croce

At the other end of the Piazza is the Basilica di Santa Croce, sitting on what used to be a marshland outside the city walls. It started as a small church but grew under the patronage of Florence's most influential families, and it is now large and full of treasures – there is a lot to see.

Just to the left of the church is a statue of Dante holding a book. Dante of course was exiled and died in Ravenna. Inside you will find his monument, but he is not buried there. Lord Byron was incensed at this omission and wrote:

> "Ungrateful Florence, Dante sleeps afar"

Although Florence tried to retrieve his remains many years later, Ravenna refused to give them up, and even hid them at one time

Have a look at the façade before you go in – it is interesting because it was put there so recently. Although the church itself is old, the façade was left as simple brick for centuries – just like San Lorenzo which you will see on walk 4.

They didn't decide to complete it until 1857, when the church decided to make Santa Croce the National Pantheon, i.e. where the greatest Italians were buried. Many famous Italians are buried here, Michelangelo, Ghiberti, Galileo, Machiavelli and Rossini...

The Jewish architect Niccolo Matas designed the church's façade and placed a large Star of David on it – right at the top and in the middle. Matas was rewarded for his work by being buried within the church grounds as he requested, but because he was Jewish he is buried in front of the main door and not actually in the church itself. Walk up to the front door to see the plaque which marks his tomb.

You have to go down the left hand side of the church on Via San Giuseppe to actually get in. Inside you find a huge bright church topped with a handsome wooden ceiling and lined on both sides by striking monuments. You can wander around freely, and it is a much pleasanter experience than the visit to the Cathedral.

From the entrance turn right to go round the church anticlockwise.

Ghiberti

This church is full of amazing tombs and monuments to Italy's finest, but oddly the artist who made one of Florence's highlights has a very simple tomb. Ghiberti was the creator of the Gates of Paradise you saw at the baptistery. So find his tombstone inlaid into the floor.

Galileo

Further down near the main door is Galileo's tomb. He was the father of astronomy, constructed his own telescope, and spotted the four largest moons of Jupiter. His patron was Cosimo II so he named the moons Cosmica Sidera – or "Cosimo's stars"; however they were also named by Simon Marius who found the moons at about the same time as Galileo. He named them after the lovers of Zeus: Io, Europa, Ganymede, and Calisto – much better.

Galileo of course was not popular with the church, since his theories shook up the idea of the Earth being the centre of the universe. Only his patron Cosimo II saved him from the stake at the hands of the Inquisition. He was forced to recant his theories and declare them "absurd, cursed and detested". Legend says that as he rose from his knees, he whispered "even so, it does move", meaning of course the Earth.

He was placed under house arrest for eight years until he died. Even then his remains were stashed away until the eighteenth century. At that point even the church relented and allowed this tomb to be constructed. In fact the church only accepted the idea that the Earth actually goes round the sun in 1992!!! Galileo is holding a telescope and gazing at the universe. The ladies represent Geometry and Philosophy.

Now cross the church to find Michelangelo's tomb.

Michelangelo

When Michelangelo died the Pope planned to host his funeral in Rome. Florence stated that he came from Florence, and that he had promised his body to Florence, so they were determined to have him. He was actually born in Capresse, but it is closer to Florence than Rome. Florence stole his body away from Rome in the middle of the night – which upset the Pope a bit.

The ladies sitting on the tomb represent the arts Michelangelo reigned in, sculpture, architecture, and painting.

Legend tells us that Michelangelo himself selected this spot so that the first thing he would see on the Day of Judgement would be the Duomo through the doors of Santa Croce.

Dante

As already mentioned, Dante is not actually in the church. His monument is however worth looking at. Dante sits on top, and the lady on the right represents Poetry who is grieving his death. The inscription at the front translates as:

Honour the Poet of the Highest Regard

Further down is the tomb of Machiavelli

Machiavelli

Machiavelli was a political scientist and his name has come to mean devious and cunning. His belief was that 'the ends justify the means' – perhaps not something everyone agrees with. The church hated his philosophy and the fact that he was so critical of religion. His books were placed on the Proscribed Index in 1559 – those are the books forbidden by the church. That list was only abolished in 1966.

He was in the government during the Medici first period of exile, and dealt with Rome and other governing bodies. He wrote "The Prince" to describe the corruption and greed he met during that time. When the Medici returned he was arrested and tortured, but managed to avoid admitting anything and was eventually released. The inscription held up by the lady means:

> So great a name requires no eulogy

Continue walking towards the altar.

Annunciation – Donatello

On your right is Donatello's beautiful stone Annunciation. This is a scene you see over and over again in paintings. Here it is in stone, but surprisingly evocative, where Mary seems to be turning in surprise at the arrival of her visitor.

There is a door on your right just past Donatello's Annunciation which will take you into Arnolfo's Cloister.

Arnolfo's cloister

Once in the cloister follow the main path to the right. It's worth walking to the end of this path just to turn round and to see the cloister at its best - the building you see at the end is the Pazzi Chapel which you will visit soon.

Return down the path and turn right before you reach the statue on the right. This will take you to the Refectory.

Refectory

This is where the monks ate under huge frescoes of the Last Supper and the amazing Tree of Life, both by Taddeo, Giotto's godson and one of his best students.

You can see that Judas sits at the opposite side of the table to Jesus and the apostles, which is where artists usually placed him so viewers would know who was who. Oddly Leonardo da Vinci didn't follow this tradition in the Last Supper in Milan. The sleeping apostle is Saint John – he is usually shown slumbering because the bible tells us he rested his head during the Last Supper.

Leave the refectory and keep right as you walk along the cloister. You will find another exit in the far right hand corner which will take you into the second cloister, Brunelleschi's cloister.

Brunelleschi's cloister

This cloister was built for the Pazzi family – but of course they never saw it – if they weren't dead they were in exile. There is a monument to Florence Nightingale under one of the corner arches. She of course was born in Florence.

Some of the scenes of the movie Hannibal were filmed in Brunelleschi's cloister!

Return to Arnolfo's cloister and keep right. A doorway will take you into the Pazzi Chapel.

Pazzi chapel

You enter the chapel under a beautiful blue dome.

The Pazzi chapel was commissioned by the Pazzi family – the same family who hatched the Pazzi conspiracy. Brunelleschi designed it but died before it was completed. Work stopped completely when the Medici family confiscated the Pazzi estate. Inside is beautiful but also quite plain - it's worth sitting on the bench which lines the wall and thinking what might have been had work continued.

Look up at the dome and you will see it has an oculus in the centre – just like the Pantheon in Rome. There are also windows around the base of the dome which lets the light stream in. Below the dome you can spot the four roundels with the four Apostles, Mathew, Mark, Luke and John.

Leave the chapel and keep right to return to the church. Once back in the church, turn right and you will find Rossini's tomb.

Rossini

Rossini has been called the Italian Mozart, and his most famous work is the Barber of Seville. He died in France and was originally buried in the Pere Lachaise Cemetery in Paris. However in 1887 the Italian government requested that his remains be placed in this church – France agreed.

As you reach the back of the church you will see a door on the right hand corner, it takes you to the Sacristy.

The Sacristy and the Cimabue Crucifix

Go through the first door on the left. Hanging here is the Cimabue Crucifix, painted in 1270. The church suffered dreadfully when the Arno flooded in 1966, and many masterpieces were destroyed or damaged. The water reached 5 meters here and this crucifix became a symbol of the disaster.

The wooden crucifix had soaked up so much water that it had expanded three inches and doubled its weight. What was left of the paint was removed and preserved, and it took years for the crucifix to return to its original dimensions. It has been restored as best possible but is so clearly damaged.

You may not have heard of Cimabue, but he is seen as the father of the Renaissance, Giotto was one of his pupils. His crucifix is seen as far more real than the previous flat and stiff Byzantine paintings – look closely to see that Jesus's hands are stretched out in pain and there is blood.

Elsewhere you will see many colourful frescoes by Taddeo – who also did the Last Supper you just saw in the Refectory.

Return to the main church and you will see a series of chapels in front of you leading to the altar. The Bardi chapel is just before the altar.

Bardi chapel

It is full of frescoes by Giotto and his students showing the life of Saint Francis. The frescoes were damaged when they decided to whitewash the chapel in the seventeenth century! In the nineteenth century they tried to repair the damage, and actually caused more damage in the process. However they are still worth a look.

The Altar

The altar itself is amazing, a kaleidoscope of Giotto frescoes and colour. These tell the story of John the Baptist.

Continue walking round the church in the same direction to reach the exit.

Amphitheatre

When you leave the church, cross the square diagonally right and go into Via Torta.

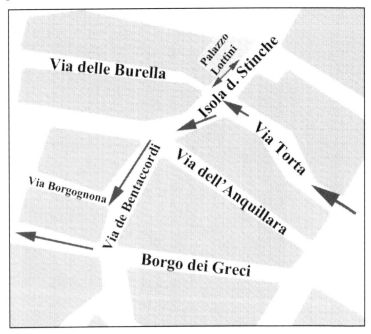

You will soon realize the reason for taking this route. This street follows the outline of the old Roman amphitheatre, as you might guess given the way it bends unlike the rest of Florence – remember Florence started as an army retirement village.

When you reach the junction with Via Isola delle Stinche turn right. Stop at number 7 on the left hand-side of the road – this is Palazzo Lottini.

Palazzo Lottini

There is a plaque here marking it as the place where sculptor Giovanni Dupre created l'Abelle Morente, a beautiful sculpture which is now in the Hermitage museum in St Petersburg

You might like to try an ice-cream in Vivoli - a much loved gelateria. Given the long walk you have just chalked up you might feel you deserve one.

Either with or without an ice-cream, backtrack along Via Isola delle Stinche to continue following the outline of the amphitheatre. You will pass Via delle Burella on your right. When you reach the crossroads with Via dell'Anquillara, continue straight ahead into Via Dè Bentaccordi.

Pass Via Borgognona on the right then take the next right into Borgo dei Greci, which will take you to the Piazza Signoria and the end of this walk.

Reward yourself with a well-deserved coffee or a drink and contemplate the treasures you have seen.

Walk 2 - Piazza della Signoria to the Pitti Palace

ClockWatching

If you start this walk early enough, you can reach the Piazza della Signoria with enough time to have a look around, before either the Palazzo Vecchio or the Uffizi open.

You should decide when you plan to visit the Uffizi (which is covered on Walk 3), and slot it into this walk if possible as it passes right by the door.

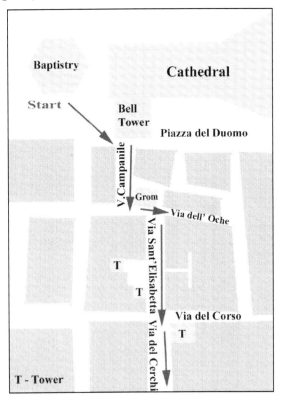

This walk starts in Piazza del Duomo. Stand facing the front of the cathedral and walk round its right hand side. When you

74

reach the Campanile/Bell Tower you will find narrow Via del Campanile on your right. Go down this little road which is a quieter route to the Piazza della Signoria than most people will take.

Grom

When you reach the corner with Via del Orche you will find Grom, a favourite gelateria on your left; it's probably too early to contemplate an ice-cream, so just remember it for later.

Turn left into Via del Orche then right into Via Sant'Elisabetta. You will soon see little Piazza della Eisabetta opening out on your right. Tucked in the corner is another old tower, the Torre della Pagliazza.

Towers

You will see a lot of towers on this walk, all belonging to Florence's wealthiest families. The reason they built up rather than outwards was tax. Tax was levied on ground space, so building upwards kept the cash safely in the family coffers.

Torre della Pagliazza

This tower is the oldest building in Florence dating from the sixth century. It is very unusual because it has a circular wall, and the reason for that is, it is sitting on the remains of a curved Roman structure which the experts think was part of a Roman baths complex. There is a little museum on the ground floor and there is a restaurant and bar in the upper levels.

By the way, the word Pagliazza means straw. It got that odd name because in the thirteenth century it became the first female prison in Florence, and the prisoners were given the luxury of straw pallets to sleep on.

The other large tower on this little square is the Torre dei Ricci – belonging to another of Florence's feuding families.

When you reach the junction with Via del Corso you will see yet another old tower on the left hand side of the road.

Torre di Croce Rosso

This is Red Cross corner and you can see two examples of the red cross against a white background on the tower. In medieval times some Italian cities voted for a Capitano del Popolo, the captain of the people, and it was his job to intervene between the common people and the ruling families. The Red Cross was one of his symbols and you will see that sign sprinkled on public buildings around Florence.

Cross Via del Corso and continue into Via dei Cerchi.

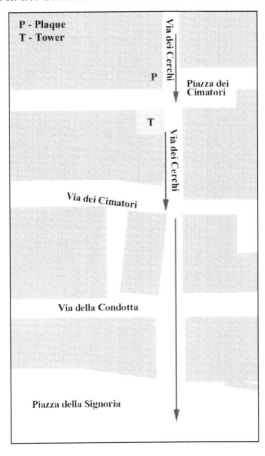

You will arrive in a little square called Piazza de Cimatori.

On the next corner on your right, at number 23, you will find a Dante plaque and a verse from The Divine Comedy. It's about Ugo, the Marquis of Tuscany, who you read about on walk 1, who gave lots of cash to the Badia Fiorentina church which is just round the corner.

Torre dei Cerchi

Cross the square to reach the Torre dei Cerchi – which belonged to the Cerchi family, the enemies of the Donati family you read about on Walk 1.

Continue along Via dei Cerchi. You will see the huge Piazza della Signoria ahead of you so just walk straight into it.

Piazza della Signoria

This is a large and busy square with lots to see. It was and still is where Florence is ruled from.

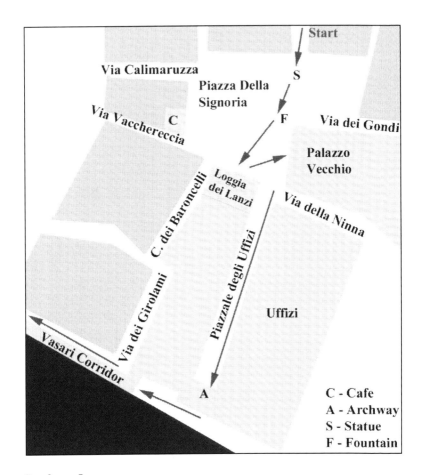

Via Calimaruzza

Piazza Della Signoria

Start

S

Via Vacchereccia

C

F

Via dei Gondi

Palazzo Vecchio

C. dei Baroncelli

Loggia dei Lanzi

Via della Ninna

Via dei Girolami

Piazzale degli Uffizi

Uffizi

Vasari Corridor

A

C - Cafe
A - Archway
S - Statue
F - Fountain

Cosimo I

As you enter the square you will see a rather grand equestrian statue in front of you. This is Cosimo I who inherited the title of Grand Duke of Tuscany in 1537 at the tender age of just seventeen. He was the only legitimate male relative of the just murdered Grand Duke, Alessandro de' Medici.

Cosimo came from a distant branch of the family, but he took to power like a duck to water, ruled completely and absolutely, and defeated all contenders to the title on and off the battlefield. The Medici continued to rule Florence until 1737 when the last of the family fizzled out.

When this statue of Cosimo on his horse was unveiled, it was admired greatly by many of Europe's leaders, who promptly ordered a similar one for themselves. It stood in this square until WWII erupted, when it was taken well away from Florence for safety. Once peace was declared, Cosimo was brought home to an ecstatic reception. Villagers lined the route and cheered as it passed in a US army vehicle. At the edge of Florence a convoy of motorbikes formed behind, and their sirens blared all the way to the Piazza della Signoria – Cosimo had come home!

Behind Cosimo I stands Neptune's fountain

The Fountain of Neptune
This fountain was installed to celebrate a Medici wedding. The sculptor was an apprentice of Michelangelo, and he chose Neptune to emphasize the ambitions of Florence to be a maritime power. Perhaps as a career move he adorned it with the face of Cosimo I.

It seems Michelangelo was not impressed with what he saw and told his apprentice

> "What a beautiful piece of marble you've ruined."

Perhaps the locals felt the same as they used the fountain as a laundry.

The Fountain has been vandalized many times over the centuries but Neptune has come through it all, if not unscathed – in 1982 he was painted bright blue to celebrate a win by the Florence football team. The final straw was in 2005 when someone tried to climb up the statue, but slipped and snapped Neptune's hand off in his attempt to break his fall. The original Neptune is now safely in the Bargello museum leaving this copy to its fate. The locals call him Il Biancone, "Big Whitey".

Beneath Neptune are Scylla and Charybdis - two sea monsters who lived on either side of a narrow channel. Ships trying to avoid one monster would fall into the clutches of the other, kind of like being stuck between a rock and a hard place. Charybdis liked to swallow a huge amount of sea water to cause a whirlpool to drag ships down. It's thought the monsters and the whirlpool were located in the Strait of Messina between Sicily and the mainland – there is actually a whirlpool there.

On the ground in front of Big Whitey you can find a round pink plaque, marking the spot where a famous execution took place.

Savonarola

Girolama Savonarola was a fire and brimstone priest, and he often harangued and mesmerized the crowds in Florence with his speeches. He was devoted to the fight against corruption, and he included the Medicis and the Pope in that category, so you could say his days were numbered.

He had visions and prophesized that an invader from the North would sweep down and cleanse the church. It just so happened that France invaded Italy at the time, so the people of Florence took him seriously. They threw the Medicis out and re-established a Republic. Savonarola, helped by gangs of religious youths, took his chance to enforce a puritanical state. His moment in history arrived when the original Bonfire of the Vanities was lit and everyone was encouraged to throw all their luxury items into it. The artist Botticelli was apparently a believer and tossed some of his masterpieces into the flames!

The Pope eventually excommunicated Savonarola and threatened to do the same to the whole of Florence. Popular opinion turned and Savonarola was imprisoned and tortured - he confessed he had made up his visions. He was declared a heretic, and this plaque marks the spot where he was hung and his body burned at the stake.

80

The painting below shows Savonarola being burned in the square – you can see it on Walk 4 in the San Marco museum.

Not everyone agreed with the verdict and the fate of Savonarola. Flowers were secretly sprinkled on this spot during the night. The tradition continues today and every year the Fiorita takes place, which involves a mass, a floral commemoration in the square, followed by a parade to the Arno where more flowers are thrown into the water – just as Savonarola's ashes were. You can find a video of this on YouTube, https://www.youtube.com.

Stand in front of Big Whitey and behind him to the right is Marzocco

Marzocco

This is a lion holding a shield with the coat of arms of Florence on it. The first Marzocco stood for centuries on this spot, but it had deteriorated so much that it was really just a lump of rock. A new version by Donatello was commissioned to replace it. Of course what you see now is a copy, Donatello's Marzocco is in the Bargello and you probably saw it on Walk 1.

Marzocco is the most powerful symbol of Florence. Where Florence went, Marzocco went. When Pisa threw off the hated rule of Florence, the Pisan crowds threw the hated Marzocco which stood in Pisa into the Arno.

Behind this Marzocco is the Palazzo Vecchio - If you stand well back and look up at the tower you can see a golden Marzocco weather vane.

Palazzo Vecchio (Old Palace)

This castle-like structure is the town hall. It has had several names in the past as it was used by different bodies for different tasks. It got this name when Cosimo I decided to move house to the Pitti Palace across the Arno – so this palace became the "old palace".

Have a look at the top windows. If you remember the outcome of the Pazzi Conspiracy from Walk 1, the Pazzi plotters were hung. Well those windows are where they were hung from, to the very vocal approval of the roaring crowd below. The bodies hung there for three days, and every now and then the keepers would cut a rope and let one of the corpses tumble to the ground. The Medici loving crowd would attack the corpse, dismember it, drag it through the town, and generally take their revenge on what was left.

Above the top windows you can see that there is a repeating sequence of nine coats of arms inset into small arches. The high tower, which you can visit later, bears a huge clock – with just one hand so you have to work out the minutes yourself. The arches at the top are open so soldiers could pour heated rocks and liquid onto any would be attackers.

To the right of the palace stands the Loggia dei Lanzi

Loggia dei Lanzi

This lovely arcade is full of statues. The Loggia was a very popular addition to the square, and Michelangelo even proposed at one point that the arches should run right around it – it's a shame they didn't follow his suggestion.

It was first built in 1387 and was where the leaders of the city made proclamations. Florence ended as a republic in

1532 when Cosimo I was proclaimed the Duke of Florence in front of it. The Loggia was then used as a station for the formidable Medici mercenaries who helped Cosimo I keep power. They were lancers – hence the name Lanzi. Later when times were safer, it was where the Medicis would sit to enjoy the entertainment or ceremonies in the Piazza

The statues look very good outside in the real world. The two at the front are the most interesting:

Perseus

The statue at the front and nearest the Palazzo Vecchio is of Perseus. He holds a sword and Medusa's head which he has just chopped off and which is oozing blood. Medusa's head is covered in snakes. This wonderful statue was cast by Benvenuto Cellini, and just to make sure everyone knew it, he engraved his name on Perseus's band which runs across his chest.

Don't miss looking at the beautiful plinth Perseus is standing on, decorated with Jupiter, Mercury, Minerva, and Diane. It's often overlooked as everyone is captivated by Perseus himself.

Walk around to the back of the statue and look at the helmet; you should see Cellini staring back at you

Rape of the Sabine Women

Still at the front but at the other end of the Loggia is the Rape of the Sabine Women by Giambologna. It is a landmark statue because it's a group statue which can be viewed from any angle. The artist created it as a test of his own skill – I think he passed.

There is confusion over this episode in Roman history because of the word rape. It actually means abduction. Legend tells us that the Sabine women were taken from their homes by the Romans who needed wives. The women then agreed to marry their abductors as free women, and even stopped a battle between their Sabine relatives and the Roman army. Sounds very like the old film "Seven Brides for Seven Brothers" although I doubt there was any dancing involved!

Moving On

Now depending on your schedule you should either move onto the Uffizi, or enter the Palazzo Vecchio.

If you don't have a specific time slot at the Uffizi and you are going to queue, or if your time slot is now, your next stop is the Uffizi. So face the Loggia again and follow it round to the left to enter Piazzale degli Uffizi. The Uffizi entrance lies on your left further down. You can read about the treasures within on Walk 3, and make your way back to this square to continue this walk later.

If on the other hand you have a later slot for the Uffizi, continue with the Palazzo Vecchio.

Palazzo Vecchio

The entrance to the palace is flanked by Michelangelo's' David (a copy) on one side, and by Hercules defeating the fire breathing Cacus on the other. Look above the entrance doorway to see two golden lions. They are guarding a Latin inscription which translates as

| Jesus Christ, King of Kings and Lord of Lords. |

Approach the corner of the Palazzo Vecchio and just behind the statue of Hercules you can spot the outline of a man's face carved into one of the stones.

84

Legend tells us that this was done by Michelangelo and there are various theories as to why he did it. One story says he did it as a dare, another that he did it with his back turned to the wall, and another that it is the face of a man being executed! Take your pick.

Go in - you can hire an audio-guide at this point to get the most out of your visit.

Cortile de Michelzzo

You enter by a beautiful courtyard known as the Cortile de Michelzzo. It is covered in frescoes which oddly depict Northern European cities: Vienna, Prague, and Innsbruck. Why? Because Cosimo I's heir, Francesco, married the sister of the Hapsburg Emperor, and these frescoes were put up as a diplomatic part of the celebrations – it was a very useful marriage!

Sadly it wasn't a happy marriage and more importantly never produced the vital result – a surviving male heir. Worse, Francesco fell in love with an Italian beauty called Bianca, and he built a palazzo for her near the family home. His wife died, probably in childbirth although foul play has been suggested. Francesco promptly married Bianca and named their son, Antonio, his heir. As you might guess, once Francesco died, his brother Ferdinando declared himself Grand Duke and Antonio was shoved aside.

In the centre of the courtyard stands a little fountain which is topped by a cherub holding a dolphin.

Cherub with Dolphin

The statue is a copy and the original is upstairs in the museum. It was by Verrocchio who was a great favourite of the Medici family - this statue was commissioned by Lorenzo the Magnificent.

It's famous because of the spiral stance of the cherub, and the fact that it can be viewed from any side – just like the Rape of the Sabine Women which you saw in the Loggia dei Lanzi. So take a walk around it. The water arrives by pipes stretching from the Boboli Gardens – which you can visit later.

Go into the next courtyard. Those huge pillars hold up the very ornamental room you will soon visit, the very grandiose Salone dei Cinquecento – the Hall of the Five Hundred.

Most of the ground floor is off- limits as the offices are still in use. So climb the huge stairway to reach the Salone dei Cinquecento. You can admire the artwork as you climb. Spot the cherubs playing with an old Medici symbol of a gold ring encrusted with diamonds, and another with cherubs playing with five red balls and the world, creating the Medici Coat of Arms.

Salone dei Cinquecento

This huge room was constructed to hold the town council once the Medici family were ousted – at least until the Medicis returned to power. At that time the room was very plain, as it was the idea of Savonarola who saw all embellishments as godless. Whilst in power the council was filled by a random selection of guild members every two months, which sounds very chaotic!

Ironically it was also in this room that the priest Savonarola was tried, before being led up the tower to be tortured until he confessed.

Labours of Hercules

Lining both walls are the six Labours of Hercules by De Rossi. The demi-god Hercules was given twelve labours but only six are shown here. They all seem to involve Hercules about to slay his enemy, and he is positively grinning while he does it in some of them.

One of the statues is the battle between Hercules and Diomedes. Hercules looks as though he is about to slam Diomedes to the floor, but perhaps he had second thoughts as Diomedes is clutching a rather delicate area of Hercules's body – you have to laugh.

You might wonder why Hercules appears so often in Florence. Well he not only killed various monsters, legend tells us he also founded various cities – and Florence claims to be one of them. This claim comes from a seal which was used on legal documents in the thirteenth century which had the image of Hercules on it. Sadly the seal did not survive.

Frescoes

Above the statues the Salone is decorated with frescos, which show Florence trouncing the neighbouring Tuscan cities. When the hall was to be decorated, the original plan was to have frescoes by the two stars of Florence, Michelangelo and Leonardo Da Vinci.

Da Vinci thought he would try a new material and mixed wax into his paint, painted a huge battle scene on the wall, and then he got impatient while waiting for it to dry. He turned on a fire to speed the drying process up, and watched in horror as the wax melted and his painting slid to the floor.

Michelangelo didn't even get his brushes out. He was summoned to Rome by the Pope, packed his paintbrushes, and set off to paint the Sistine Chapel.

So the frescoes you see now were done by Vasari and his school – not quite so well-known but it's still an amazing room. Vasari's frescoes depict Florence conquering all; you can see the Florence lily on the flags of the winning armies.

There is a theory that Leonardo's painting is still partly in existence. One of the frescoes shows the battle of Scannagillo. It's on the wall opposite the entrance door and is the second fresco on the left. Look at the back and you will see a group of soldiers and a flag emblazoned with:

CERCA TROVA

which means:

Seek and ye will find

Vasari was a great fan of Leonardo da Vinci, so some historians think he was trying to mark the spot where the painting lies. But it's only a theory.

Michelangelo's work does make an appearance with the statue Genius of Victory on the right of the door you entered by. It was actually made as part of a papal tomb but Cosimo I liked it so much, he had it brought into the Salone instead.

The ceiling

Find the central panel of the ceiling – and you will see Cosimo I looking down at you as he is crowned.

Studiolo of Francesco

From the door you entered by, turn right and you will find a little room further down the same side of the Hall. As already mentioned, Francesco was the heir of Cosimo I and this is where he would retreat from the affairs of state.

This little room is decorated with sumptuous paintings and statues. Each wall represents one of the elements. From the door you entered by, the paintings behind you represent Earth, to the right Fire, to the left Water, and the furthest away Air.

You might notice that the paintings are either of gods and goddesses doing godly things, or more interestingly people discovering or inventing – glassworks, bronze-works, alchemy, gunpowder, the list goes on. Francesco was a bit of a dabbler in science himself and behind the paintings are cupboards where Francis stashed his experiments and his collection of scientific oddities. Amongst his prizes is a unicorn horn, but I think we can assume it came from some living creature. Usually such claimed unicorn horns turned out to be from the narwhal, a tusked whale found in the Arctic Ocean.

Francesco actually discovered how to make Porcelain, that exotic material which Europeans imported from China and paid so much money for. Obviously if anyone could find out how the Chinese did it, they could potentially make a fortune. Francesco experimented endlessly and seemingly found a method, although his product was not really as fine as the Chinese. His workshop marked the various items with an image of the Dome and the letter "F". There is a piece in the National Gallery in Washington. When Francesco died his discovery died with him – and it wasn't until the early eighteenth century that the secrets slipped out of China and into Europe.

Behind you and above the entrance is a painting of Cosimo I – Papa, and on the other side of the room is Eleanor of Toledo – Mama.

Also take a look at the wonderful statue of Apollo, on the right hand side at the back – it's by Giambologna - the same chap who did the Rape of the Sabine Women which you saw in the Loggia dei Lanzi.

The paintings on the back wall also give access to secret passageways to other rooms in the palace. You can purchase a "tour" to be taken through the secret passageways – ask in the ticket office if you are keen.

The Palazzo is still used as the Town Hall, so most of the other rooms on this floor are off limits. So now climb up to the second floor. You will wander between the private apartments of the Medici family and imposing public rooms.

The Quartiere Elementi suite.

These rooms are on your left from the top of the staircase. They were the private rooms of Cosimo I, and the walls are decorated with depictions of the four elements, fire, earth, water. The ceiling depicts air.

The Terrace of Saturn

From the Suite of the Four Elements, pop out onto this little terrace for a view over Florence.

The Hercules Room

This room is decorated with various scenes of Hercules and his Labours.

However if you are a science fiction fan you should have a look at the painting in this room, officially called The Madonna and Child with the Infant St John. Unofficially it's called The Madonna and the Flying Saucer. In the background you can see what looks like a flying saucer, and below it there is a man and a dog gazing up at it in wonder. The official interpretation is that it is an angel, but I prefer the UFO theory.

Sala Verde

The rather ugly door in this otherwise pretty room is the entrance to the Vasari corridor, the shortcut built for the Medici's stretching from here to the Pitti Place across the Arno. Another tour you could consider will take you through that door and along the corridor.

Cappella di Eleonora

This little chapel was for the private use of Cosimo I's Spanish wife Eleonora and is worth pausing in. It is covered in frescos of biblical scenes portraying the Story of Moses. The left wall shows us the dramatic Parting of the Red Sea, where the Jewish people are safely on shore, and the Egyptian army is drowning – you can recognize them by their helmets.

Udienza

This room has an amazing golden ceiling which took six years to complete. It is laminated in pure gold and must have cost a fortune. The walls are full of colourful frescoes.

Hall of Lilies

This beautiful room gets its name from the blue and gold ceiling – covered in the symbol of Florence, the Lily.

Judith and Holofernes

Here you will find Donatello's Judith and Holofernes. The bible tells us that the Jews were under attack by the King of Nineveh, Holofernes. The Jews were under siege and famine threatened. Beautiful Judith crept into the enemy camp, seduced Holoferenes, plied him with drink, and then chopped his head off. She carried the head home to show her people and give them courage. The Jews won the battle.

The statue catches the moment of Holofernes's death as Judith raises her sword high. Holofernes lies dead at her feet.

Sala delle Carte Geografiche

Another room worth visiting is Cosimo I's Map Room. Here you will find cabinet panels decorated with maps of the world, as the world was known at the time – no Australia. You can even see Mexico and California! There is a plan at the door which will guide you to any map you are particularly interested in.

Behind each door lies part of Cosimo's collection of artefacts from the area on the cabinet door. Finally right in the middle of the room is the monumental globe which was originally lowered from the ceiling when Cosimo wanted to have a look. It's very worn now, but must have been fascinating when the world was still being explored and discovered.

Tower

You can also climb the palace tower, the Torre d'Arnofo, which has 418 steps. It's a great view but be warned they only let 25 people up at once – so you may have to queue. The entrance is just next to the ticket office.

The tower has two cells which housed Cosimo the Elder before he was exiled, and then later Savonarola the priest, who was burned at the stake.

The tower is also a bell tower, and inside is Martinella. This bell used to hang in an old church which burned down long ago. The Florentine army took the bell into battle – but before the army set off, Martinella was rung for thirty days to warn both the people and the enemies of Florence that battle was coming – no surprise attacks then! Later Martinella was used to summon the people to the square. It fell silent throughout World War II, but rung out in defiance in 1944 to raise the people to oust the Nazi's who were in retreat.

Leave the Palazzo and consider if you would like a hot chocolate! Opposite the Palazzo is Caffè Rivoire, one of Florence's loveliest and most expensive cafes.

Caffè Rivoire

This café was founded by Enrico Rivoire, a Court Chocolatier from Turin, who followed the royal family to Florence when it was briefly the capital of Italy. It was a great success, and the Florentines have been coming in for chocolate ever since. You could try the wonderful hot chocolate, or just remember the café for later at the end of the walk.

Facing the Loggia dei Lanzi, go round its left hand side to reach Piazzale degli Uffizi. Walk past the Uffizi, unless you choose to tackle Walk 3 at this point. Go down this narrow street to the river. Turn right to walk along under Vasari's corridor.

Vasari's Corridor

The Medici's lived in the Pitti Palace on the other side of the river, but they had to attend to business in the Palazzo Vecchio. Rather than having to mingle with the common people, Grand Duke Cosimo I ordered the elevated walkway above you to be built. It runs from the Palazzo Vecchio, past the Uffizi, along the river where you are now, crosses the Ponte Vecchio which you can see in front of you, and stretches to the Pitti Palace!

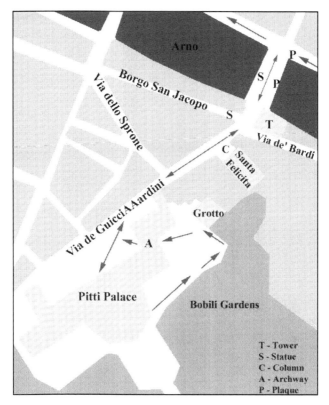

Carry on till you reach the Ponte Vecchio on your left. Just before you cross the bridge find the plaque with a quote from Dante on the archway on your left:

> Conveniasi a quella pietra scema
> Che guarda il ponte, che Fiorenza fesse
> Vittima nella sua pace postrema

Or in Longfellow's translation:

> But it behoved the mutilated stone
> Which guards the bridge, that Florence should provide
> A victim in her latest hour of peace

Ponte Vecchio

The original bridge was wooden but it was swept away by the Arno in 1345 and this lovely stone replacement was built.

Merchants have always traded here, although originally they used tables rather than shops. Legend has it that the word bankrupt comes from this bridge. When a merchant went broke his table (banco) was broken (rotto) by soldiers. Of course it is just a legend not fact – but who knows?

Originally the butchers traded here, but when Vasari's Corridor was put up, they were quietly displaced so that Cosimo I would not be offended by the sights and smells. The jewellers moved in. Nowadays when you walk across it you will find tourists and lots of expensive jewellery shops, so you may not want to linger. If you have the chance, visit the bridge again very early in the morning to see it without the hordes.

Do stop at the middle of the bridge which has some archways open to the river – without them you would not know you are on a bridge at all. There is a plaque on the left hand side of the bridge at the end of the open archways. It commemorates Gerhard Wolf who was the German consul in Florence and saved many Jews from the horrors of the camps. In 1955, he was made an honorary citizen of Florence.

There is yet another Dante plaque just next to it. It reads

IN SUL PASSO D'ARNO

which means

At the crossing of the Arno

The bust standing in the middle of the bridge is Cellini, the sculptor who produced the wonderful Perseus you saw earlier. An odd tradition started late last century - young lovers placed a padlock on the gate of this memorial to seal their love and then tossed the key in the Arno. Florence did not approve of this, removed most of the padlocks, installed a warning at the

96

front of the fence, and imposes an on the spot fine of fifty euros if you are caught. The lovers did stop and now just come to touch the padlocks which are still there.

Once over the bridge spot Torre dei Mannelli on your left – you will have to move to the right of the bridge to see it as it is not very tall.

Torre dei Mannelli

This is the only surviving tower of the four which used to defend the corners of the bridge. It even withstood the might of the Medicis when the Mannelli family refused to have it destroyed to make way for the Vasari Corridor. Instead the corridor swerves around it. Well done the Mannelli family!

Just opposite the tower, on the corner of Borgo San Jocopo and at the base of the Torre de Rossi Cerchi is the statue of Bacchus. Although the Germans decided to spare the Ponte Vecchio they made sure that the Allies couldn't use it. They blew up just about everything around it. This tower and most of the buildings were rebuilt from the rubble, and Bacchus was placed here.

Take the second left to pass under Vasari's corridor into Piazza San Felicita.

Piazza Santa Felicita

You will find a granite column in this little square. It used to have a statue of Saint Peter the Martyr at the top but it fell off in the eighteenth century. It is a commemoration of a battle between two religious groups in the thirteenth century; one led by Saint Peter the Martyr. The column was badly damaged by the retreating Nazis as they lay waste to the approach to the bridge, but it was restored.

Behind the column is the entrance to the church of Santa Felicita

Santa Felicita

It's thought to be the second oldest church in Florence, the oldest is San Lorenzo. It's from the third century and it's named after Saint Felicity of Rome. She was a martyr who refused to give up her religion, even after each of her seven sons was martyred one by one!

If you have time and energy, and if the church is open, pop in. You can see the Vasari Corridor which actually runs along the church and has a large opening where the Medicis could attend church without having to mingle with the commoners down below.

Find The Deposition by Pontormo which is generally seen as a "masterpiece". It's in the first chapel on the right. It's very blue, and surprisingly bright and modern for a painting from 1528!

Below the church runs an underground passage which was originally the main road to Rome. Below the cloister is one of the city's first Christian cemeteries.

When you exit, continue left to walk along Via Dè Guicciardini and it will open up into another tourist hot spot, Piazza de Pitti

Piazza de Pitti

This square gives access to the Palazzo Pitti and the Boboli Gardens. Enter the palace courtyard by the high central archway on your left.

Palazzo Pitti

If you have a Firenze card you should visit the bookshop to get your card swiped and receive your receipt before you start climbing the stairs to the museums. The bookshop is on the other side of the courtyard you entered by. If you don't get your receipt you will just be sent back down again to get it.

The Palazzo Pitti was started by the ambitious and wealthy banker Luca Pitti. Pitti became the right hand man of Cosimo the Elder and was lavishly rewarded for his help and loyalty. With all his new wealth and power he decided to build this palace, to rival anything the Medici's had – his aim was to have it dwarf the Medici palace. He didn't live to see it completed and later his family, who needed the cash, sold the palace to Eleonora de Toledo, the wife of Cosimo I as she wanted a family home! The Medici's then expanded it, built the Boboli gardens, and lived there for generations. It was the largest palace in Europe until the Palace of Versailles was built.

Later Napoleon moved in, and finally the Italian Royal Family during that period when Florence was capital of Italy. The palazzo was then given to the people by King Victor Emmanuel.

It has six museums inside, and you will simply not be able to see everything. So again choose what you find most interesting. The main museum is the Palatine Gallery on the 1st floor. The museum holds works by Raphael, Rubens, Botticelli, Caravaggio, and many, many others. You can explore it all if you have time, but try to find the following highlights.

Prometheus Room

This room has frescoes showing Prometheus stealing fire from the Gods and giving it to mankind - and suffering the terrible consequences. This is the room where the Council of the Grand Duchy sat.

Madonna and Child – Fra Lippi

This is one of the most loved paintings by the amorous monk Fra Lippi. In fact tradition states that the model for the beautiful Madonna in this painting was none other than Lucrezia, the nun who was seduced and eloped with Lippi.

Technically the painting is important because the viewer sees depth - especially on the right hand side where Lippi used linear perspective. Artists made lines converge to a single point in the distance - like railway tracks disappearing into the distance.

Madonna and Child and the Young St John the Baptist - Botticelli

100

In the same room you will find this beautiful painting, which is fitting as Botticelli was a pupil of Fra Lippi. In fact he even travelled to Hungary to complete a fresco ordered from Fra Lippi's workshop by the archbishop of Hungary.

Room of Jupiter's education

Sleeping Cupid – Caravaggio

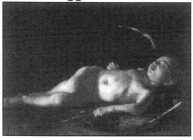

Caravaggio used light and darkness to set the mood of sleep and night – so unlike the light and movement you usually associate with Cupid, who is usually depicted as dashing around with his bow and arrow. Caravaggio actually completed this painting whilst he was in Malta, on the run from a murder charge in Rome!

The Saturn Room

This room is full of Raphael's so if you are a fan you might want to linger

The Vision of Ezekiel – Raphael

This is very dramatic. Ezekiel has a vision of God on a throne. The throne is constructed of a man, an ox, a lion, and an eagle. These are the traditional symbols of St Matthew, St Mark, St Luke and St John. God speaks to Ezekiel who stands in the ray of light.

This painting was stolen by the French in 1799, but returned when Napoleon was defeated.

The Jupiter Room

The ceiling is decorated with nymphs and cherubs.

La Donna Vetta- Raphael

This is one of Raphael's best works. According to rumour, the veiled woman was Raphael's lover, the daughter of a baker

from Siena. If that story is true, it is quite comical to think of a baker's daughter looking down on the mighty Medicis. Raphael died at just 37, supposedly after a night of particularly torrid sex with his girlfriend.

Mars Room

This room hosts more than one Rubens:

Consequences of War – Rubens

This painting was one of Rubens later works and it shows the folly of war. It was his attempt to dissuade his government from getting involved in the catastrophic Thirty Year War which laid waste to large parts of Europe. Flanders still went to war.

The Four Philosophers – Rubens

Rubens painted himself (far left), his brother (next left), and two friends as the philosophers. In the background you can see the Palatine Hill of Rome.

Apollo's Room

Penitent Magdalene - Titian

Titian actually produced several versions of this painting, some with Mary dressed and some not. After the crucifixion Mary Magdalene went into the desert for the rest of her life and repented. Legend says that her clothes fell off and left her only with her hair to cover herself.

Napoleon's tub

Napoleon did conquer this part of Italy, and stayed for some time in this Palace. This was his totally over the top tub room.

Boboli Gardens

Return to the courtyard to find the entrance to the gardens.

Now the gardens are mostly just large green areas so don't visit expecting a vista of pretty flowers. It's worth at least a quick visit for the view of the Cathedral dome, but if your time is limited you might want to skip the garden altogether.

The gardens were for the private use of the Medici family, and Cosimo I's wife Eleonora designed them. To keep all the greenery green, a conduit was built from the Arno and irrigates the entire garden. Remember the dolphin fountain you saw in the Palazzo Vecchio, well the water feeding it comes from these gardens.

From the Palace follow the path up to the left and you will see the Cathedral dome above Florence. Turn right to go uphill just a little to see the obelisk and the garden stretching out over a hill in front of you. You can wander uphill if you have the inclination.

Turn left and follow the path downhill with the Cathedral in front of you. The path eventually double-backs towards the Palazzo but before it does, you will find the Large Grotto on your right which you should have a look at.

It was commissioned by Francesco Medici. It is totally man-made, decorated with stalactites, and originally had water features. It's dry now. When it was first constructed it had an opening to the skies to let the light in, which would then reflect off the fountains.

The Grotto used to house the original Michelangelo's Prisoners which you will see on Walk 4 – they were later stashed in the Academia for safety leaving us with copies instead. Follow the path towards the palazzo and you will enter the main courtyard again.

When you leave the Palazzo turn right to return to the Ponte Vecchio which you should cross again.

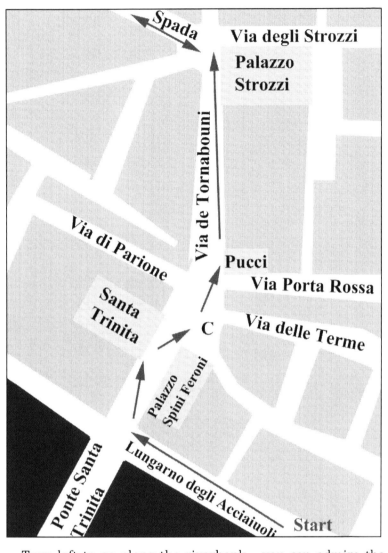

Turn left to go along the riverbank - you can admire the Ponte Santa Trinita in front of you as you do.

Ponte Santa Trinita

Pause when you reach the Ponte Santa Trinita.

This beautiful bridge is not a tourist trap like the Ponte Vecchio. It is the oldest elliptic arch bridge in the world. It was built by Ammannati, the same artist who sculpted "Big Whitey" who you saw in Piazza Signoria, but unlike his fountain, this bridge was appreciated and much loved. The statues guarding both ends represent the seasons - Autumn and Winter are on this side of the river, Summer and Spring are on the other.

Sadly the Nazis did blow this bridge up, but Florence fished the original stones out of the Arno and rebuilt it in 1958. It took them a few more years to find and restore the head of Spring. If you get the chance, walk along the river at sunset to enjoy this bridge at its best.

If you were to cross it and walk along a few blocks you would find the Palazzo di Bianca Cappello, the home of the Italian beauty who caught the heart of Francesco di Medici. For now though turn right to walk along Via dè Tornabuoni

Via dè Tornabuoni

This is the place to go if you want fashion. The street is named after another of Florence's great families, whose most famous members were two very beautiful and intelligent women, Lucrezia and Giovanna – they both married into the Medici family. So it's very apt that this most glamourous fashion street is linked to two of Florence's most glamourous women. This street is also the home of the church of Santa Trinita on your left.

Santa Trinita

This church was the family church of the Strozzi family. Florence had many wealthy and powerful families, and second to the Medici family was the Strozzi family, one of the richest banking families in Florence.

Palla Strozzi was a liberal thinker and in his later years managed to get Cosimo the Elder exiled in 1434, but Cosimo soon returned to power and reciprocated by exiling Palla – he died in Padua never seeing Florence again.

His son managed a reconciliation with the Medicis and started to build the beautiful Strozzi Palace which you will see soon. However things took a turn for the worse when his son Filippo Strozzi led an uprising against the Medicis – even though he had married Clarice de'Medici. In fact Filippo was involved in the creation of Florence's last republic. But once again the Medicis returned and Strozzi fled to Venice. He later tried one more time to overthrow the Medicis but was foiled and in the end he killed himself. Later generations also seemed to meet nasty ends, usually on the wrong side of a battle. A sad family really.

Outside their family church is a Roman column which came from the Baths of Caracalla in Rome and which was given to Cosimo I by Pope Pius IV, who was a distant member of the Medici family. It took more than a year to get the column from Rome to Florence, and the ship carrying was attacked twice by Turks on route.

Cosimo was keen to put his own image on top, but decided to be more subtle, so it is topped by a statue of Justice and has Cosimo's name at the bottom – perhaps as a reminder of who was in charge. The Medicis decided the perfect place to put the column was outside the Strozzi family church, and near the Strozzi Palace which is just a few blocks away. That's really rubbing salt into the wounds.

If the church is open pop in. It was built by the Vallombrosian monks – not a name you are likely to have heard of. It has many chapels and they are bursting with art.

Spini Chapel

This chapel is on the left hand side about half way down. It is worth a look for the wooden statue of Mary Magdalene which was clearly inspired by Donatello's Magdalene which is in the Cathedral Museum and which you might have seen on Walk 1.

Sassetti Chapel

This chapel is the highlight of the church – you will find it at the back to the right of the altar.

The wealthy Sassetti family, who commissioned the "Story of Saint Francis" frescoes, is depicted in several of the frescoes.

Have a look at "St Francis Receiving the Role of Orders from Pope Honorius" which is near the top. It is interesting, not for the events being depicted but because you get a window into Medici times. The Palazzo Vecchio and the Loggia dei Lanzi which you have just visited fill the background.

The cast is interesting. Spot dark-haired Lorenzo the Magnificent on the right – he is always easy to identify.

Coming up the stairs are his children, Giuliano, Piero, and Giovanni – you can see the curiosity of Giuliano at the front, looking out at you the viewer. Giovanni at the back became Pope Leo X.

Below it is the "Resurrection of the boy" which is the one with the little boy sitting up and looking very healthy. In the background you can see what had just happened, the boy tumbled out of a window perhaps chasing his red ball which is on the ground. The fall is fatal, but he is brought back to life by Saint Francis as depicted in the foreground. This miracle actually took place in Rome, but has been moved to Florence in this fresco – in fact it's situated outside the church you are standing in. The boy is seen falling from the Palazzo Spini which is opposite the church, so you can compare how it looked then and now when you go outside again. Also in the background is the Santa Trinita Bridge so again you can see how it looked centuries ago.

Finally at the bottom is the altarpiece which shows a very pretty Virgin Mary with a soft veil over her hair in The Adoration of the Shepherds. You can see the Magi arriving in the background.

The altarpiece is flanked by the figures of Sassetti and his wife. Sassetti paid for the whole thing and he and his wife are buried beneath it.

Doni Chapel

To the left of the Sassetti chapel is another little chapel and in it you will see a crucifix of which there is a story. It's called the San Giovanni Gualberto's crucifix, because Jesus is said to have nodded his approval to San Giovanni when he forgave his brother's assassin. In front of it is a crystal reliquary which is said to hold a piece of the column that Jesus was tied to when he was whipped

Sacristy

110

The Sacristy is to the right of the Sassetti Chapel. Before the Strozzi family was ousted the sacristy was their chapel. It used to house a masterpiece, The Adoration of the Magi by Gentile da Fabriano, which was commissioned by Palla Strozzi. However it is now in the Uffizi, so you may have seen it earlier. The sacristy is now full of art saved from the 1966 flood.

Palazzo Spini Feroni

Opposite the church to the right is the very grand Palazzo Spini Feroni; Feroni was a rich cloth merchant and banker. He bought this piece of land from the monks of Santa Trinita and built this palace. Over the years it has been a hotel and shops have been housed in it. It was finally bought by a shoe designer in the thirties, Salvatore Ferrangamo, and today it is a shoe museum. So if you have a love of shoes you might want to pop inside. It rotates the display among the 10,000 shoes he designed.

Back outside turn towards the column and continue down Via de Tornabuoni. Have a look at the very expensive Pucci store on your right at number 20. Pucci is another old Florentine family and you will see their palazzo on walk 4.

This road has many beautiful palazzos along it, and one worth going into is the Palazzo Strozzi further along on your right.

Palazzo Strozzi

This was the family home of the Strozzi family until last century, when Florence took it over. It's now used as an exhibition space – so you need to check what is on when you visit Florence to see if you are interested:

http://www.palazzostrozzi.org

It has a nice courtyard where you can sit down for a welcome refreshment if needed – or you can hang on as you will be visiting a few cafes shortly.

Walk to the next junction. On your left is a fork and you should go down the right hand side into Via della Spada. Walk a little way down to the Caffè Giacosa on your right at number 10.

Negroni Cocktails

This used to be the Caffé Casoni, which is where the Negroni cocktail was invented. One night Count Negroni asked the barman to use Gin rather than soda water in his usual cocktail as he wanted a bit more of a kick – and the Negroni was born. The original Casoni café closed and for a while it was an exclusive antique shop, but has reopened as Caffè Giacosa. So perhaps you should return in the evening and try it.

It has a literary connection – James Bond orders a Negroni in the original "For your eyes only" story. It was also much loved by Orson Wells and he is said to have described it:

> "The bitters are excellent for your liver; the gin is bad for you. They balance each other."

If you like gin you might enjoy trying one out.

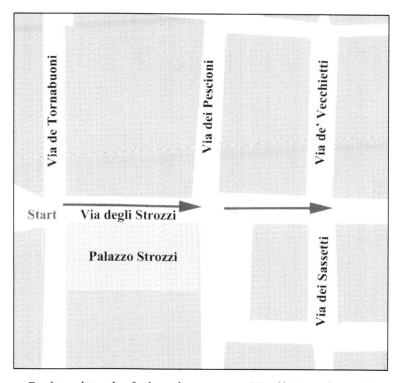

Backtrack to the fork and cross over Via dè Tornabuoni into Via degli Strozzi. Ahead of you is an archway and it will take you into Palazzo Repubblica so head towards it. Pass Via dei Pascioni on your left, but pause for a moment when you reach the junction with Via de' Vecchietti also on your left.

The Devil

On the right hand corner you will see a little statue of the devil. This marks the spot of an old legend.

In the thirteenth century Saint Peter the Martyr was preaching against heretics in Piazza della Repubblica – which is the square just through the archway ahead of you. A black horse went wild with hooves thrashing at the crowd. The saint declared it was the devil and held his arms out to turn himself into a cross. The horse turned and raced away down this street where it disappeared. The devil marks the spot.

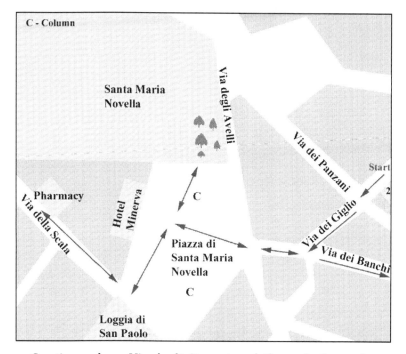

Santa Maria
Novella

Via degli Avelli

Via dei Panzani

Start

2

Pharmacy

Via della Scala

Hotel
Minerva

C

Via dei Giglio

Via dei Banchi

Piazza di
Santa Maria
Novella

C

Loggia di
San Paolo

Continue along Via degli Strozzi and through the archway into the centre of the square beyond it. The archway is a triumphal arch, built to celebrate the moment that Florence became the capital of Italy – but Rome took over just five years after.

Piazza della Repubblica

This square was where the Roman forum stood – the supposed exact spot is marked by the Column of Abundance. It was crossed by two Roman roads, the Cardo and the Decumano.

The Forum was replaced by the Ghetto and a market. The Jews were originally invited into Florence by the government, because the local money lenders charged huge amounts of interest and the Jews would charge less. They were given free rein of the city and despite a restriction on their interest rates they amassed a great fortune.

However once Cosimo I took power their days were numbered. He played the political game and pandered to the prejudices of the banking families. So he enforced laws which have a horrible ring of familiarity about them some centuries later. They had to wear specific clothes, were banned from all trade including money lending. Finally the Ghetto was built to restrict their movement. Not surprisingly any Jewish family, who could, left, leaving behind the poor.

The Ghetto was swept away in the nineteenth century when Florence was briefly the capital of Italy. All the old medieval towers, churches, and homes were razed – so sad. Even the old city walls which once ran alongside were torn down. They planned to carry out the same modernisation over more of the city, but thankfully it stopped, partly due to an international outcry.

Today it is home to Florence's street artists, and is a fun place to go in the evening. The square has a little carrousel which tinkles away in the background. On Thursday nights there is a flower market

There are some cafes around the square which were frequented by the writers and artists of old. You will find Café Gilli and Caffé Paskowski on the left hand side of the square. Caffé delle Giubbe Rosse is on the right hand side.

Caffé Gilli

The first Caffe Gilli was opened in 1733 by the Gilli family from Switzerland. In the 1920's it moved to this location on Piazza della Repubblica and is decorated in the Belle Époque style. It was a popular place for the intelligentsia who debated in the café. It is full of antiques and chandeliers in beautiful Murano glass from Venice.

Caffé Paskowski

Caffé Paskowski was founded in 1846. It has Art Deco floors and walls, and is so beautiful it is used for fashion shows. They still follow the old tradition of chanteuses singing to the guests

Caffé delle Giubbe Rosse

Caffé delle Giubbe Rosse is named after Garibaldi's Red Shirts, and they are honoured in the traditional uniform of the waiters, red jackets. This was a hot spot for intellectuals between the wars. Its walls are covered in photos and drawings from those turbulent years.

After enjoying your refreshment stand with your back to the archway, walk cross the square and turn right to leave by Via Calimala.

Take the next left Via Orsanmichele.

Orsanmichele

The church on your right gets its odd name from the fact that it was built on the kitchen garden of St Michael, a church which has long gone, and the building was actually a grain store to start with. This explains it's very unchurch boxlike shape. The ground floor was a loggia like the other loggias you have seen on these walks – with arches and columns and no actual walls. Grain was bought and sold in the loggia and stored and dispensed from in the upper floors.

So why was it transformed into a church? When you go inside you will see the reason - a painting of The Madonna of the Graces which is elaborately enshrined. It's said that the grain traders had visions of the Madonna near the painting.

Before you go in though, if you have the energy and time, continue along Via Orsanmichele to walk right around the outside of the church. The exterior is decorated all around with niches containing statues – each one put up by a different guild. The niches really show the competitiveness of Florence's guilds, all trying to outdo each other.

The richest guilds, the Bankers guild, the Wool guild, and the Cloth guild, all had enough cash to commission an expensive bronze statue, whereas the rest made do with stone. The Merchants guild commissioned Verrocchio's Doubting Thomas - Thomas is shown checking if the wounds are real! The Armorers and Sword-makers commissioned Donatello's St George, and the original is now in the Bargello so you may have already seen it. Of course the statues you see outside today are copies, the originals are inside the church in the museum –they are also being restored back to their original glory. You will eventually return to the front of the church in Via dell'Arte della Lana.

Entrance to the church is free so if it's open pop in for a look round.

As well as the painting, you can still see evidence of its original use as a grain store by the chutes in the pillars – where the grain was dispensed.

If you happen to visit on a Monday you can also visit the museum, which is housed in the old granary store-rooms, and see the original statues now sheltering from outside.

When you leave the church/museum, turn left to go down Via dell' Arte della Lana. Turn right along Via dei Lamberti and finally left down Via Calimala. Ahead of you is the Mercata Nouvo

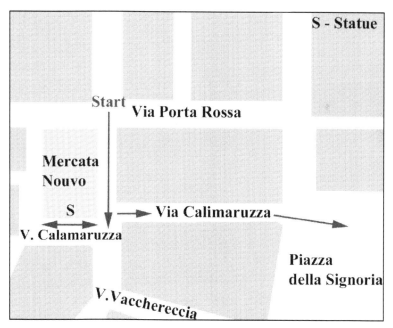

Mercata Nouvo

This is another old covered market full of stalls which you can browse around and perhaps find a bargain. It's centred round another Loggia which used to be the silk and gold market.

Next to the loggia is a fountain and a much loved statue of a boar, the boar is known as Porcellino, or Little Pig – it's a copy of a Greek statue you might have seen in the Uffizi. If you want some luck, put a coin in his mouth, rub his nose and if the coin drops into the grating in front of him you will be lucky. I expect some civic department gathers the loot up at some time.

Right in the middle of the Loggia there is a marble slab with a chariot wheel engraved on it - but it will most likely be covered by market stalls. The chariot wheel was from a Caroccio, a special chariot used when Italian cities went to war. The army suspended a bell and the city banner from the chariot which was driven by four white oxen. It was placed in the middle of the army in the midst of battle as a symbol of the city and guarded by the army's finest – its loss was catastrophic.

On one of the rare occasions neighbouring Lucca went to battle, they defeated both Florence and Pisa, and as a humiliation the Caroccio of both cities were pulled backwards into Luca.

If the battle was won, the captured Caroccio was given into the safe keeping of the family which distinguished itself best in battle. If you climbed up the Palazzo Vecchio tower on Walk 2 you will have read about Martinella, Florence's war bell.

For some reason, this round stone engraved with a chariot wheel became known as the Stone of Shame and is where merchants who went bust were humiliated before going to prison. Their trousers were pulled down and they were beat on the buttocks until they fell onto the stone.

Face Porcellino and turn right to leave the market by Via Calimaruzza to return to Piazza Signoria. If you haven't yet had a refreshment, you could always head to Caffè Rivoire for a hot chocolate.

Walk 3 - The Uffizi

This walk covers the Uffizi which you will have to fit into your schedule as queues and booked time slots allow.

The Uffizi

Even if you have been organized enough to just walk straight into the museum, take a moment to look at the palace it sits in – on both sides of the road you are walking down. Uffizi means "offices" which is what this building was. Francisco, the son of Cosimo I, had it erected to house the cities magistrates, but it soon became a treasure trove of the Medici collections.

When the final member of the Medici family died, she gave the whole shebang to Florence on condition that it never leaves Florence. The collection has been on display since 1765. It has not been without disaster. In 1966 Florence was flooded and terrible damage was done.

As you walk down Piazzale degli Uffizi you will pass a gallery of statues of the artists and architects who worked on and adorned Florence. See how many names you recognize – try again at the end of your visit to Florence and you will probably recognize quite a few more.

When the Uffizi was built the alcoves now hosting these statues were vacant. Florence wanted to fill them with her famous artists, but that meant sculptor's fees and costly marble, an expensive business. They tried various financing schemes before finding the solution – a lottery. They effectively appealed to the greed of the city's population, and soon the money was pouring in and the statues were churned out.

Now go into the Uffizi. There is so much worth seeing in this museum that you absolutely must decide what you want to see before you go in. The museum is split onto two floors and you will start on floor two which holds the Renaissance paintings – it is the busiest area so expect to shuffle along and queue to see the highlights. You will then go down to the first floor which is still full of amazing paintings, but will be quieter. Partly because a lot of people just don't have the energy for it and also a lot of the "groups" will skip it.

You will find crowds around the main paintings, but remember that large paintings are often seen best by standing back, so try it before queuing up for a closer look. When you need a break, head for the rooftop café and you might manage to squeeze in!

There is usually some redevelopment going on in the Uffizi so some rooms may be closed and paintings may be on the move. If one of your favourites is not on show, it always gives you an excuse to visit again on another holiday.

No doubt you will have your own ideas of what to see, but here are some personal favourites and suggestions. Note the locations cannot be guaranteed but where possible they are listed in room order at the time of writing.

La Sala del Duecento e di Giotto – Thirteenth century and Giotto

Byzantine – Renaissance – what's the difference

At the start of your exploration you will come into a room with three large paintings of Mary and Jesus. All three depict exactly the same scene but are by three different artists and show nicely how art leapt from the Byzantine style to the Renaissance style.

The three artists are Cimabue, Duccio and Giotto. Giotto is seen as the first great renaissance artist and if you compare his version to the other two you can see the difference – his is the middle one. Giotto started to infuse some real expression and life into his paintings, whereas Byzantine is flat and motionless.

La Sala del Trecento Senese – Fourteenth Century Sienese

Annunciation by Simone Martini and Lippo Memmi

This is a stunning painting glowing with gold. It is an early work from the fourteenth century by two brothers-in-law. You can see their names at the bottom. The archangel Gabriel has just landed and is telling Mary what is to come. To be honest Mary looks decidedly unhappy by the prospect.

This painting seems much more delicate than the paintings you just looked at next door.

Sala del Gotico Internazionale – International Gothic

Adoration of the Magi - Gentile da Fabriano

This painting is full of glowing gold and opulence. It was commissioned by Palla Strozzi for the Santa Trinita church – if you have already completed Walk 2 you will recognize that name. The Strozzi were enemies of the Medici, and incredibly rich – hence the amount of gold in the painting!

The top panels show the Three Kings in the East seeing the Star of Bethlehem. Next they enter Jerusalem to be met by Herod, and finally they arrive at Bethlehem. The main panel shows the Magi in the process of removing their crowns and placing them at Christ's feet. The king wearing red stockings is having his spurs removed before he approaches – and it cleverly looks 3D. The ladies behind Mary are examining one of the gifts just received.

Fra Lippi

124

Madonna with Child and two Angels - Filippo Lippi

This artist was orphaned and placed into a monastery by his aunt – most probably for her own convenience. Lippi was not really suited for the religious life, and often skipped prayers, preferring to draw.   Eventually his superiors suggested he study art.

He left the monastery but was still bound by his vows; however that didn't stop him having many lovers. He made his living by painting for various churches. He then fell in love with a novice in one of the churches, Lucrezia Buti.   He seduced her and they eloped, despite the nuns efforts to claim her back. He continued to paint and even teach - Botticelli was one of his pupils.

Here he has painted a beautiful Mary and it's generally thought that he used Lucrezia as his model. The painting has an oddly Flemish look to it – from the cityscape in the background to Mary wearing pearls and a veil on her hair. The angel at the front seems to be looking right at the viewer.

Duke and Duchess of Urbino - Piero della Francesca

This is a very famous painting, even if its creator is not so well known.

The Duke and Duchess are in profile, mostly because the Duke of Urbino lost his right eye and gained a broken nose in a tournament. The Duchess has an unhealthy pallor, perhaps because she was actually dead when the painting was produced. It's believed the artist used her death mask as a model.

Botticelli

Birth of Venus – Botticelli

This painting was caked in aged and dark varnish until it was carefully cleaned and restored.

Here Botticelli illustrates the arrival of Venus into the world from the sea. The story portrayed was inspired from another work which was painted for Alexander the Great by Apelles in ancient Greece. That painting did not survive beyond the Roman Empire and Botticelli used only its description as his guide.

Venus's shell is pushed along by the wind gods Zephyr and Aura, entwined around each other on the left – figure out whose legs are whose! As Venus arrives she is showered with roses and a nymph is ready to cover her with a cape. Botticelli cleverly illustrates the blowing wind by Venus's hair, the cloak, and the leaves of the trees, all in motion. Look at her beautiful billowing hair

La Primavera – Botticelli

It's thought that Primavera was commissioned by the Medici family as a wedding gift to a family bride. It's full of mythological figures.   On the left is Mercury opening the clouds to bring in spring. In the middle we have Venus, the goddess of love, and the Three Graces - Chastity, Beauty and Love. Cupid hovers above the scene. Venus is wrapped in a myrtle plant which symbolizes marriage, love, and children.

On the right is Flora the goddess of flowers. Flora was raped by Zephyr the Wind God, who was then ashamed of what he had done, so he married Flora and made her the goddess of flowers. You can see Zephyr blowing flowers onto Flora to transform her into a goddess.

The garden is full of flowers and blossom - all very productive. Spot the oranges which symbolize the fruit of marriage, i.e. children.

There is no record of what the bride thought when presented with this painting, but she certainly knew what was expected of her - offspring!

Adoration of the Magi – Botticelli

You might first just glance at this and think, another nativity scene. Well that is certainly correct, but take a moment to look at the cast.

The Magi are the three central kneeling figures facing Mary. Botticelli used the faces of Cosimo the Elder and his two sons, despite the fact that they were all dead when the painting was produced. The proud figure standing on the left is Lorenzo the Magnificent, the ruling Medici at the time.

Now look to the lower right hand side, the young man facing out towards you is in fact Botticelli. Still on the right hand side but further in is an older man also facing towards the viewer. That is the banker who paid Botticelli to paint this altarpiece.

Annunciation – Botticelli

This is another religious painting where Mary gets the glad tidings from the Archangel Gabriel. This painting is very different from the golden version you saw earlier.

Calumny of Apelles – Botticelli

This is not a very famous work but it is worth spending a few moments on. Botticelli has recreated an ancient painting called Calumny which was also painted by Apelles in ancient Greece, and which Botticelli once again reproduced by description only.

Midas sits on the throne with his asses ears, into which Ignorance and Suspicion are whispering. Hatred stands before the king with a club, and behind him is Slander dragging a young man behind her. Fraud and Deceit are prettifying Slander. Behind this group is a sad Penitence and behind her is Truth – who looks a lot like Venus from La Primavera.

Apparently Apelles painted this scene because of a slander against him from another artist, but we don't know if Botticelli was himself slandered when he decided to recreate it.

Leonardo

Annunciation – Leonardo da Vinci

Here is Leonardo da Vinci's take on the Annunciation.

Da Vinci spent a lot of time trying to figure out how flight was possible. Gabriel has been given wings which are quite different from the beautiful long feathered wings you normally see in religious paintings. These wings were probably modelled on birds – so perhaps da Vinci was actually figuring out how an angel could fly.

Take a look at Mary's arm resting on the podium. It looks odd because the podium is much closer to the viewer than Mary is, and couldn't actually be in the painted position. Leonardo da Vinci was only in his twenties when he painted this, and everyone makes mistakes. Or did he? One theory is that this painting was supposed to be seen from the right hand side. Step back to the right and your view of the painting will shift, bringing Mary's arm into the correct position. We don't know if this was the case, but da Vinci certainly studied perspective.

One other point, da Vinci's fingerprints have been found on the painting, apparently he used his fingers rather than a brush on occasion.

La Tribuna

This octagonal room is a treasure in itself and has recently been restored. That beautiful dome is encrusted with 6000 mother of pearl shells from the Indian Ocean. The Medicis placed their most treasured statues and artworks here. It's too precious to allow the hordes of tourists in so you will need to wait at one of the doors for your chance to peep in.

Venus

Venus stands in the Tribuna. This Roman statue was at one point the star of the whole Uffizi – all those rich Europeans doing the "Grand Tour" wouldn't have missed her. Nowadays she doesn't really stand out from the crowd, and you can't really get a good view of her from the doorway.

Michelangelo

Doni Tondo- Michelangelo

Here is the holy family, but with a strangely masculine Mary. It's thought that this was because Michelangelo used a male model. It's worth remembering this fact for your visit to the Medici Chapels on Walk 4 as you will see another example of Michelangelo's strangely masculine female figures.

Durer

Adoration of the Magi – Durer

This is a cheerful scene, as once again the Magi present their gifts to Christ. The three Kings are dressed opulently and the landscape is lush. There are even some butterflies bottom left – a butterfly is a symbol of the Resurrection.

Parmigianino

Madonna with the long neck – Parmigianino

This painting gets its odd name simply because of the Madonna's swan like neck; in fact all her limbs are elongated. She has an elaborate hairstyle and is wearing pearls and beautiful clothes – all highly unusual.

Mary is accompanied by four angels and again all the figures are strangely elongated. Except Saint Jerome, who is on the right hand side of the Madonna and is tiny - very odd. The whole painting seems out of balance.

Veronese

Martyrdom of Saint Justina – Veronese

Cyprian lusted after the virtuous Justina and tried to seduce her, but her faith was too strong. Eventually Cyprian gave in and also became Christian. That did not please the local ruler who had them both captured and tortured to make them revert to the old pagan gods. When that failed he passed the problem to Caesar who ordered that they both be beheaded.

Portrait of Count Giuseppe da Porto with his Son Adriano – Veronese

This painting is a family scene and you can see the love and affection between father and son – quite unusual as most family paintings show no emotion at all between the subjects. Also the rich clothes they are wearing look so real you want to touch them.

16th to 18th Spanish Painters

133

St. John and St. Francis – El Greco

As always El Greco's figures are elongated and almost emaciated. Here a storm gathers behind the two Saints.

Raphael

Madonna of the Goldfinch – Raphael

If you are a student of art you will spot immediately that Raphael has placed the Madonna and the two boys, Christ and John the Baptist, in a triangle. However most of us will just see a young and beautiful Madonna, the two boys, and the colourful setting. Christ's foot rests on his mother's, which is a tender touch.

The Goldfinch held by John the Baptist is a symbol of the crucifixion. Legend tells us that a goldfinch tried to remove a thorn from the crown of thorns and was splashed by Christ's blood, giving it the red markings we know today

Titian

Flora – Titian

This beautiful woman is Flora, the goddess of flowers. Titian was famous for his love of red, so here he has adorned Flora with golden red hair.

Venus of Urbino – Titian

Venus lies on her bed and gazes back at the viewer – very different from the shy Venus by Botticelli. It was commissioned by the Duke of Urbino as part of a clothes chest for his bride to be - a traditional Italian wedding gift – perhaps to encourage her on their wedding night. You can see such a chest in the background which is being searched by some maids. The little dog sleeping beside Venus symbolizes fidelity; you will often see a dog in portraits of wives or lovers.

Over the centuries this painting has been dismissed and lambasted by prudish critics. In fact Mark Twain hated it. He said:

> "You may look your fill upon the foulest, the vilest, the obscenest picture the world possesses; Titian's painting of the Venus d'Urbino. It isn't that she is naked and stretched out on a bed; no, it is the attitude of one of her arms and hand"

Apparently even Mark Twain's complaint was censored by the American press!

Caravaggio

Bacchus – Caravaggio

Bacchus is of course the God of wine and revelry. Here we see him as a teenager wrapped in a sheet and having had one too many. You might notice that this God seems to be left – handed. Caravaggio used his own hand as a model, so since he had to paint with his right hand, the god had to use his left hand. Caravaggio also leaves a warning on the fleetingness of youth, in the overripe fruit which is past its best and getting a bit wormy. Also look at the leaves of the fruit, so beautifully painted.

When the painting was cleaned at the start of the twentieth century, a little portrait of Caravaggio was found on the surface of the wine in the carafe bottom left – but you won't be able to see it. The experts restored the picture and unfortunately the little picture merged into the background, so now it needs special lighting to be visible. There is talk of restoring it again to bring it out.

The painting was commissioned by Cardinal del Monte who was reputed to host parties with many young men in attendance – the cardinal commissioned many paintings of this sort which seem to reflect his taste.

Sacrifice of Isaac – Caravaggio

Everyone knows this story, Abraham is ordered to sacrifice his son Isaac to prove his faith. Caravaggio has painted the moment just before the sacrifice, when an angel grasps Abraham's arm to stop him. Look at the fear and terror on Isaac's face. With the other hand the angel points to a handy nearby ram which should be offered instead. The artist uses light and shadow to dramatize the moment.

Medusa – Caravaggio

The Medusa was of course a Gorgon from Greek Mythology. There were three gorgons who all had snakes for hair, and would turn you to stone if you looked at them. Medusa was

137

defeated by Perseus who used his shield as a mirror to battle with her. Caravaggio has painted Medusa's head which is still alive after the decapitation. Medusa's horrified expression displays her own fear in her last minutes.

Bronzino

You can't fail to notice the painting of Nano Morgante. Cosimo I wanted to emulate the great houses of Europe so he employed a dwarf as court jester. The name Morgante was given to him in a joke – it's the name of a giant from an Italian poem. Cosimo both humiliated him and rewarded him – but overall life was probably better in court than life outside court for a dwarf.

Bronzino painted him from the back and the front, and Cosimo was so pleased with the result that the painting was hung in the Palazzo Vecchio. Once Cosimo was gone, the painting was quietly stashed in another of the Medici villas and forgotten about. The villa then became a girl's school, so some brushwork was applied to Morgante to cover him up with fig leaves. Its final indignity was being put in a museum cupboard.

It saw the light again in the 1980's and restoration was undertaken. The restorers debated whether the fig leaves should be removed, and considered what they might be left with. However once the fig leaves were removed, they

138

discovered that the dwarfs modesty was maintained by a butterfly. The restoration took over twenty years.

It's thought that the painting originally stood in a revolving frame letting the viewer see both sides of Morgante by the flick of a wrist. Today's viewer has to move around to see both sides.

Judith and Holofernes – Gentileschi

This shows Judith dispatching Holofornes – another scene which you will see more than once as you explore. This is a very bloody version. The artist was a woman from the seventeenth century, a time when women artists were practically unheard of. Perhaps she chose this story to paint, as it was also about a woman who did not conform to the norm.

The Jews were under attack by the King of Nineveh and the army was led by General Holoferenes. The Jews were under siege and famine threatened. Beautiful Judith crept into the enemy camp, seduced Holoferenes and got him drunk, then chopped his head off. She took his head home and lifted it up high to show her people that the enemy could be defeated. The Jews took courage and won the battle

This painting is full of light and shadows. It shows quite graphically the strength and effort involved in decapitating someone with a knife. It takes all the effort of Judith and her maid to hold Holofernes down.

139

You might need a coffee and a rest now, and you could try the roof café.

You will exit at the back of the Uffizi, so to get back to Piazza Signoria just keep left and after two turns you will walk along Via Della Ninna and you will see the Loggia dei Lanzi ahead of you.

Via della Ninna

As you do you will pass a small wooden door on the side of the Palazzo Vecchio. It gives access to a secret passageway in and out of the Palace. It was put there by the ruler of Florence in the thirteenth century, a Frenchman named Gualtieri di Brienne.

That was a time of murder and mayhem, when the Guelphs and Ghibellines were at each other throats. Brienne was a tyrant and rode roughshod over the mighty banking families, so perhaps he foresaw that they would try to get rid of him. He finally took fright and escaped Florence via this door.

You could continue with Walk 2 if you interrupted it to visit the Uffizi.

Walk 4 - The Accademia

Clock watching

The San Marco church and museum are only open in the morning Monday to Friday, so if you are a Fra Angelico fan, you need to get there before noon to have time to look around. It's open all day on Saturday and Sunday

Once again you start this walk in the cathedral square.

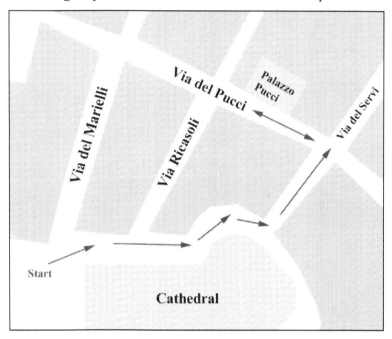

This time start by facing the Cathedral door, and go round to the left of the Cathedral. Pass Via Ricasoli on your left, then leave by the next road, Via dei Servi. Take a short detour by turning left into Via dei Pucci.

At the corner you will find a bricked up window. It was sealed by Cosimo I to mark a plot by the Pucci family to assassinate him. Pandolfo Pucci was sacked from Cosimo's court for immoral conduct and planned his revenge. Cosimo often passed this point as he made his way from the Palazzo Medici to the Santissima Annunziata church, and the plotters planned to murder him from this window. They were caught and both the assassins and Pandolfo Pucci were executed.

Continue down Via del Pucci and on your right you will find Palazzo Pucci at number 4.

Palazzo Pucci

This is the only palazzo in Florence still owned and lived in by the original family – lucky family! The Pucci were one of Florence's original banking families, and like the other great families, they were patrons of the arts – they commissioned works from Botticelli which are now in the Prado in Spain.

Look up to see the family logo, a black Moor's Head wearing a headband – rather unusual I think. But not that unusual it seems, the previous Pope, Benedict XVI, also sports a Moor's Head on his coat of arms as shown below.

You can enter the courtyard which houses various expensive shops but you can't actually get inside the Palazzo – as well as home, it's also the headquarters of the Pucci fashion business.

142

The family's most recent famous member was Emilo Pucci who designed for Hollywood stars such as Princess Grace of Monaco, Jacqueline Kennedy, Audrey Hepburn, Elizabeth Taylor, and Marilyn Monroe. There are Pucci exclusive boutiques around the world, including of course Florence. You would have seen the Pucci store in Via de' Tornabuoni on Walk 2.

Backtrack to Via dei Servi.

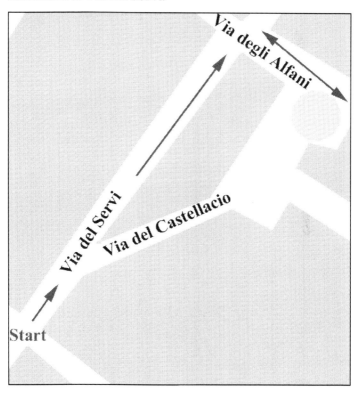

Turn left and pass Via del Castellacio on your right. Take a little detour by turning right into Via degli Alfani to find the Rotonda di Santa Maria degli Angeli.

Rotonda di Santa Maria degli Angeli

This often overlooked little building was an oratory to the nearby church. Take a walk around to the front to see it at its best. It was designed by Brunelleschi, the creator of the Cathedral's dome, and construction started in the fifteenth century. Unfortunately Florence went to war with Lucca about the same time and the funds earmarked for the oratory were diverted to the conflict. So it was left unfinished and was nicknamed Il Castellacio - the broken-down castle. It finally got a wooden roof stuck on it in the seventeenth century, a bit of a come down from the planned dome.

It deteriorated through the years and was only saved in 1936 – although its current restored architecture is not quite what Brunelleschi envisioned. The university owns it now

Return to Via dei Servi and turn right to continue to reach Piazza della Santissima Annunziata.

Palazzo Grifoni

Take a look at the pink palazzo you pass on your left as you enter the square. This is the Palazzo Grifoni, where the Grifoni family lived for centuries. It was commissioned by Ugolino Grifoni, who was secretary to Cosimo I.

Ugolino sent his own ship to the battle of Lepanto in 1571 – that battle was one of the most significant battles in European history. For once the European countries stopped fighting each other and stood together to face the invasion from Turkey. Battle fleets from, Genoa, Tuscany, Venice, and Spain converged at Sicily and headed east. The European fleet defeated the Ottoman invasion of Europe at Lepanto in Greece – if they had failed everything we know in Europe today would have been very different. Ugolino Grifoni's ship was the Tuscan flagship in that battle.

Now stand in the square and turn to look at the top floor of the palace and notice that the rightmost window is open. It's never closed. Another of the sons of the Grifoni family was just married when he was called to war. His wife waited by that open window for years clinging to hope, but she finally died an old lady. The family then closed the window but a whirlwind came from nowhere, disrupted the room and blew it open again – and it's been left open ever since.

Less romantically, the chap on the horse is one of the Medici clan; Grand Duke Ferdinando I. Ferdinando was the son of Cosimo I and inherited after his brother died. He was one of the Medici's more popular Grand Dukes. The statue was cast from enemy cannons from a North African battle.

Take a look at the rear of the statue. You will see an odd carving – it's a queen bee surrounded by an army of worker bees. It's supposed to represent the Grand Duke in the centre of the hard working Florentines. Traditionally Florence's children are brought here to count the number of bees as a way of learning their numbers. The going rate is about one minute to get the right answer.

To the left of Ferdinando is the Ospedale degli Innocenti.

Ospedale degli Innocenti

The name commemorates the massacre of the innocents as Herod hunted for the baby Jesus. The Hospital of the Innocents was an orphanage, originally under the patronage of the Silk Guild whose members were immensely wealthy. They used some of their riches to care for the poor and unwanted children of Florence – and there were a lot of them. It's estimated that 375,000 babies were given into care over five centuries! That's roughly 750 abandoned babies a year.

The building on the right is the orphanage and was designed by Brunelleschi. Look just above the arches to see the series of blue roundels where the orphans are symbolised by ten babies in swaddling clothes. Interestingly one of the babies is shown with the swaddling clothes falling away but no-one knows why.

At the far end of the arcade is a door which used to host a rotating wheel against a window, which let the parent of an unwanted child send the baby into the hospital without being spotted. You can see the window the babies would enter by. The plaque underneath it translates as

For 4 centuries this was the wheel of the Innocents, secret refuge from misery and shame for those to whom charity never closed its door

The abandoned babies were retrieved on the other side and cared for – usually given straight into the arms of a wet-nurse. The first baby arrived on February 5 1445, and was named Agata Smerelda after Saint Agatha whose feast day that was.

The boys were given an education and the girls were taught to keep house. The girls had a choice of marrying or becoming a nun, although later in the sixteenth century they did allow the girls to do neither and remain in residence.

The hospital suffered financial problems just like hospitals today. They had to hire wet nurses to actually feed the babies, which was expensive. This had the result that some mothers would become a wet-nurse to earn the extra cash at the hospital, and then feed their own infants with cow's milk!

The wheel was decommissioned in 1875 but the orphanage continued and took in destitute children during both world wars.

The building is undergoing some much needed restoration and while it is being restored, the museum is still partially open for visitors but the paintings are not on view. Ask at the desk and if the paintings are still not in view, skip it and continue from the Santissima Annunziata.

The museum has some interesting items which reflect the building's history. There are some interesting paintings showing the care of the children:

- Mary protecting Children - Domenico di Michelino
- Instruction of the orphans – Bernardo Poccetti
- Prayer in the Dormitory – Bernardo Poccetti
- The Visit of Cosimo II de Medici - Bernardo Poccetti

The building today houses the Istituto degli Innocenti which studies and advises on the care of children.

Santissima Annunziata

The Piazza's church lies directly opposite your entry point to the Piazza. Before you go in look at the tiles along the front porch - right in front of the main door you will see another example of the Moor's Head, part of the family crest of the Pucci family whose palace you saw at the start of this walk. They built this beautifully columned porch.

The church itself was founded in 1250. Just two years later, Brother Bartolomeo tried to paint The Annunciation but abandoned it because he couldn't make the Virgin's face beautiful enough, and he fell asleep. Yes you guessed it, when he woke it had been painted by an angel. The church became famous and was named after the miraculous painting.

Pilgrims flocked here and started to leave wax offerings, and some went so far as to leave life size effigies of themselves – there was even one of Lorenzo the Magnificent. The church added an atrium, the Chiostrino dei Voti, to the front of the church to display them in. The pilgrims and later the tourists loved it. It's a pity that in 1786 they melted the lot down and turned them into candles.

The Basilica della Santissima Annunziata was also where the villagers from around Florence gathered to celebrate the Immaculate Conception – the day the Virgin Mary conceived. They brought harvest foods and set up a market in the square. So if you are in town on the evening of September 7th, you might see the modern day version, a procession of families carrying lanterns and lead by a band, walking from Piazza Santa Croce to this church. It's called the Festa della Rificolona

Enter the church and in the atrium take a look at the fresco on the right hand side. It's by Francesco di Cristofano who was nicknamed "The Franciabigio". It shows the Marriage of the Virgin Mary. Franciabigio poured his heart and soul into this painting, but the friars apparently got impatient and uncovered it before it was completed. Franciabigio was so angry that he attacked the Virgin and damaged her face. You can see the mutilation.

Inside the main church you will find the miraculous painting of The Annunciation on your left, and you might also find lots of flowers in front of it. Florence's brides visit this church after their wedding to give their bouquets to the Virgin.

You will be drawn to the ornate Tribune which holds the altar. The Tribune has ten sides containing eight chapels. The chapel right at the back was designed by Giambologna for his own tomb. You will have seen many of his works already - remember The Rape of the Sabine Women?

On the left hand side of the church you will find the door to the cloister. Turn right when you enter the cloister to reach the Chapel of St Luke. He happens to be the patron saint of painters, and many Florentine artists took this to heart and were buried here – including Cellini who created the wonderful Perseus in the Loggia dei Lanzi. Franciabigio who defaced the Virgin in this church is also here – it's a wonder the friars allowed him back in, even if he was dead.

Leave the square by standing with the church directly behind you and turn right along Via Cesare Battisti.

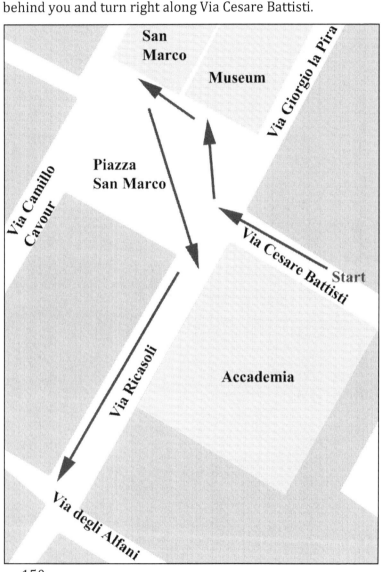

This will take you along the side of the University, and into Piazza San Marco. Once you reach the Piazza, take a look at the church on your right.

San Marco Church

This church had two famous priests. One gained fame as a marvellous artist, Fra Angelico - you may have spotted his works in the Uffizi. The other gained fame for quite different reasons, Savonarola who was burned at the stake as a heretic and who you read about on Walk 2 in Piazza Signoria.

Fra Angelico was one of the first friars to work at the brand new San Marco - and he was commissioned by Cosimo Vecchio to fill it and the convent next door with his paintings. Inside the church you can see the altarpiece. It's listed as one of Angelico's masterpieces.

San Marco Museum

Just next door in what was the convent is the San Marco Museum. Fra Angelico filled the monk's cells with paintings. Strangely, Cosimo Vecchio had his own cell in the convent for those days when he wanted to escape from it all – although of course his cell was much bigger than the average monk's cell.

When Savonarola arrived there during his brief spell in power, he moved into the Medici cell. You can have a look at

151

the painting by Dolciati which shows us Savonarola being taken to be burned in Piazza del Duomo.

Take a walk around the cells to see the Fra Angelico paintings and to have a look at some relics of Savonarola.

The Last Judgment shows the good praying on one side, and the wicked being tortured on the other.

A highlight is The Annunciation which is at the top of the staircase. It's a dramatic sight as you climb the stairs.

When you leave, cross the piazza diagonally to the left to leave by Via Ricasoli. Not far down on your left you will reach the Accademia.

Galleria dell'Accademia

This is another tourist hotspot where there is more than one queue, so if you have the Firenze card, make sure you get into the right one.

The Academy was the idea of Grand Duke Leopoldo who wanted to centralise Florence's art schools and fill it with old masters to encourage the students. This is the result.

The main reason for visiting it is to see the real statue of David by Michelangelo, the one standing outside the Palazzo

Vecchio is of course a copy. The original arrived here in 1873. There are however many other items worth a look.

The Hall of the Colossus

You will enter by the Hall of the Colossus. This room holds a model of the Rape of the Sabines which you saw in the Loggia Lazio on walk 2. As explained earlier, this statue was built to be viewed from any angle so walk right around it and decide for yourself.

St. John the Baptist, Mary Magdalene – Fra Lippi

This rather distressing painting is by Fra Lippi and we see John the Baptist and Mary Magdalene. Everyone knows that John the Baptist liked to starve himself and go into the desert to find God, but according to the church so did Mary Magdalene after the crucifixion – this is despite the fact there is not one mention of this in the bible. Most likely the church didn't know what to do with her so they added this bit of history to tidy up.

The Madonna of the Sea – Botticelli

The painting gets its name because of the ocean background. Jesus is holding a pomegranate – Botticelli often painted the Virgin Mary or Jesus holding a pomegranate because of its bright red contents are supposed to represent the suffering of Jesus.

The Prisoners

The Hall of the Prisoners forms a grand entrance towards the star of the show, David. However don't just march through.

On either side of you are four male nudes, looking as if they are trying to push their way out of the enclosing marble – hence the name The Prisoners. They are called Waking Slave, Bearded Slave, Young Slave, and Atlas.

153

They were started by Michelangelo for the tomb of Pope Julius II – who wanted to go out in style. The plan was to have forty statues in that tomb. Michelangelo went to Carrera where the best marble is quarried and personally chose the blocks he wanted. Unfortunately the money ran out and work stopped, the Pope died and his grand plan went with him.

After Michelangelo's death the unfinished statues were found in his workshop by his heir. They were placed in the grotto in the Boboli gardens which you might have visited already. They were moved into this museum in 1908.

Bust of Michelangelo – Volterra

Also in this room, just before the Prisoners, is a bronze bust of Michelangelo by one of his pupils Volterra. It's thought to be the best likeness we have, but he does look very sad.

David

It's carved out of a single piece of marble and was originally intended to adorn the roof of the cathedral as part of a series of 12 biblical statues.

Michelangelo didn't actually start this statue, two other sculptors worked on it but abandoned it as too difficult, and 25 years later Michelangelo took up the challenge. It took him two years to complete. It was decided that the task of raising a six ton statue to the top of the cathedral was impossible, and there was a long discussion on where it should be placed – finally deciding on the Piazza della Signoria. It took six days to transport the statue from the workshop to its new home where it stayed for centuries before arriving in this museum. Like many beautiful items it has been attacked. In 1991 David's left foot was damaged by a hammer wielding lunatic.

In 2010 a light replica was hoisted on the cathedral roof just for one day – the only chance to see how it would have looked if the original plans had been followed – you can see photographs in the museum.

If you look at it long enough you will be struck how large David's head, hands and feet are – this is apparently because if the statue was at the top of the cathedral, large appendages were needed to be seen from the ground. Look closely at those hands and you can see the veins, also on David's neck. David looks worried doesn't he, it seems the statue shows David preparing to battle with Goliath, so perhaps he had cause to worry.

It's clearly worth a great deal of money and Florence is still fighting the Italian Culture Ministry which claims ownership. Even if they get it, what are they going to do with it – put it in Rome?

Florence liked to identify itself with David, an independent city with powerful enemies all around. The statue is orientated so that David is glaring at Rome, as if daring Rome to threaten Florence.

The Tree of Life - Pacino di Bonaguida

This is one of the Accademia's least known but most important treasures.

We see the crucifixion on the Tree of Life. It has twelve branches which represent the twelve tribes of Israel. On the twelve branches are little pictures showing key scenes from Jesus's life. Some of the paintings are rather odd, so look closely.

Right at the top is a pelican pecking at its own breast to feed its young – another grisly representation of the crucifixion and the sacrifice of Jesus.

Further down there are some odd-looking black demons taking the condemned down to hell. One of the little pictures has a beam of light transporting Jesus to heaven where he reappears as a tiny Jesus at the neck of the Virgin in another picture. Across the bottom you can see the story of Adam and eve, and finally right down at the bottom of the tree is the devil sitting in his cave.

When you leave the Galleria, turn left into Via Ricasoli. You will reach the junction with Via degli Alfani. This street got its name from the Alfani family who were bankers but made the same mistake as Dante in backing the White Guelph party, and like him they were exiled from Florence.

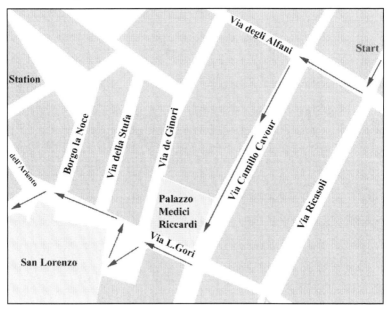

From Via Ricasoli turn right into Via Degli Alfani then turn left into Via Camillo Benso Cavour. As you approach the next junction you will find the huge palazzo Medici Riccardi on your right.

Palazzo Medici Riccardi

When you reach the nearest part of the Palazzo, look up to the first floor and you will see a little terrace – an unusual feature in Florence.

Also along the ground level are ancient torch holders with attached rings which visitors could hitch their horses to. As you turn the corner don't miss the beautiful old torch holder on the corner of the Palazzo.

This palace was commissioned by Cosimo the Elder when he first became Duke of Tuscany, and he lived there for some time. Later it became the home of the less prominent members of the family. The building was later sold to the Riccardi family, so as you explore you will see both the Medici coat of arms and the Riccardi coat of arms.

It has a beautiful courtyard, a little lemon garden, and the highlight is The Chapel of the Magi. As you explore the rooms don't forget to look up at the ceilings – they are always decorated and worth a look.

The Chapel of the Magi

Climb the staircase to reach the chapel and see the masterpiece it holds - Benozzo Gozzoli's frescoes of the 'Procession of the Magi" across three walls. These paintings transpose the story of the Three Wise Men to Florence, and the artist places himself and the stars of the Medici family in the scene.

The Three Wise Men who found Jesus in Bethlehem were Caspar, Balthasar, and Melchior.

On one wall, Caspar leads the procession on his white horse, dressed in white with red stockings. It's thought this is supposed to be Lorenzo the Magnificent – even though all other paintings of Lorenzo show him having jet black hair. Right behind him with a red hat and also on a white horse is his father Piero the Gouty – who did indeed suffer from gout. Next to him on a donkey is the founding father of the dynasty, Cosimo Vecchio.

Behind that group is a who's who of medieval Italy, each of the figures is represented by some dignitary not just of Florence but also the other powerful cities in Italy.

Oddly Lorenzo appears again in the painting; in fact he is in the crowd of red hatted young men behind Cosimo Vecchio, this time as a young boy. The artist himself stands behind him and looks straight at you. He's the one whose red hat has some writing on it.

Bearded Balthazar is on the next wall also riding a white horse with a magnificent crown and is thought to be the Byzantine Emperor John VIII.

Melchior, who is the oldest of the wise men with white hair and beard, wears red and is on a donkey. There is a debate on exactly which King/Emperor/Prince is portrayed but the money is on Joseph II the Patriarch of Constantinople.

Sometimes there is so much colour and detail in a painting that it is difficult to actually focus on anything and so much is missed. So try to take in the shimmering jewels, luxurious fabrics, gleaming birds and of course the angels – the artist used very, very expensive materials such as lapis lazuli and gold leaf to get those effects.

You have to admire the self-belief of the Medici – a family of bankers portraying themselves as the Magi with the monarchs of Europe!

By the way, the sacristy on both the left and the right have secret exits – perhaps for emergencies in those tempestuous times.

You should also explore the Galleria which is on the first floor. It glows in gold from floor to ceiling and looks over the little garden.

The last gem on the first floor is the stunning library.

Leave the Palazzo and turn right to continue down Via Cavour. Turn right at Canto de Medici, or Medici Corner. This will take you into Via L Gori, and as you walk along you will pass the palazzo garden wall on your right – far too high to see over!

You will reach a square which is dominated by the church of San Lorenzo.

San Lorenzo

The original church on this spot dates from the fourth century so was older than either the Baptistery or Santa Reparata (the church the Cathedral was built over).

Cosimo the Elder ordered the church to be rebuilt in the fifteenth century, but the first thing that will strike you is that it looks a bit rough and ready – that's because the façade was never completed and was left as brick. If Michelangelo's design of white Carrera marble had been followed it would have been stunning. In fact there were discussions afoot of actually completing the church to Michelangelo's design – but it's all conjecture at the moment.

Regardless of its exterior, it is more than worth a visit inside, so go through Donatello's gorgeous door, ornately engraved inside and out.

159

The Pulpits

The church is a Donatello treasure trove. From the main door walk straight down the aisle to find the two pulpits which were done by Donatello and his school. One of them depicts Savonarola's fire and brimstone sermons which Donatello was witness to.

Donatello's Tomb

This lies in the transept (the church crossing) on your right hand side. Donatello was still at work on the main door of this church when he died

Saint Lawrence

Left of the pulpits is a colourful fresco which shows the legend of St Lawrence who the church is named after. The Roman authorities ordered Lawrence to hand over the church treasure. Lawrence promptly gave any valuables away to fellow Christians. When he was hauled back to the authorities a large crowd followed, and when asked about the treasure, Lawrence told the Romans that the worshippers behind him were the only treasure the church had – Rome was not amused and executed him, but it an appalling way. They roasted him alive. Legend tells us that at one point he said to his torturers,

> "Turn me over; I'm done on this side"

but the church does not confirm it. Amusingly St Lawrence is the patron saint of chefs!

To the left of the fresco is the Martelli chapel.

Martelli chapel

It holds the sarcophagus of Niccolo Martelli the chap who started the Accademia which you visited earlier to see David. The sarcophagus is very unusual in that it takes the form of a wickerwork basket and was by – Donatello!

Annunciation – Filippo Lippi

Lippo Lippi wooed his women by giving them everything he owned, and then if the lady still refused him, he would paint her portrait to shake off his lust. Legend says that he was finally poisoned by the relatives of one of the ladies he seduced.

Once again we have one of the figures looking at us and pointing to what is being painted. This is an unusual Annunciation as the story only speaks of the archangel Gabriel, and there is no account of two of his pals being there as well.

Now enter the Old Sacristy. The entrance is diagonally left as you exit the Martelli chapel.

The Old Sacristy

After Cosimo the Elder's death, Florence named him Pater Patriae, "Father of his Country" which you can see carved upon his tomb on the left of the door you came in by.

Look up to the small dome above the altar to see the night sky on 4 July 1442. That date marked the arrival of Rene d'Anjou in Florence. Who? Well he was the king of Naples and is now seen as a good influence on Cosimo the Elder. Cosimo was persuaded to embrace the arts for everyone; he opened the first library in Europe and instructed the University to

161

offer Greek. Suddenly Italians had the chance to understand Greek and with that democracy and other Greek theories and beliefs.

As you leave the Sacristy, look to your left. Here is the monument to Countess Moltke-Hwitfeldt San Lorenzo, who is interesting for her name alone. It shows an angel sweeping the countess up to heaven, with the countess's hair showing the movement.

Modern Art

Back in the main church Find Pietro Annigoni's "Saint Joseph and Christ in the Workshop" where it looks like Jesus is getting a carpentry lesson. It's the one of the very few modern paintings you will see in Florence. If you face the altar it's on your left hand side.

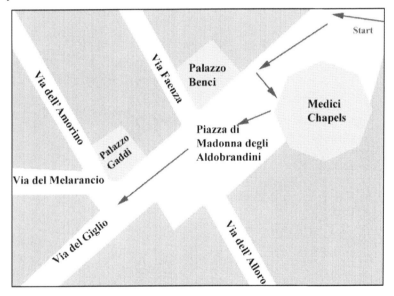

The Medici chapels are attached to the church but you can't reach them from inside. Instead exit and turn left to go round the back of the church to reach Piazza Madonna degli Aldobrandini and find the entrance.

Before you go in take a look at Palazzo Benci directly across from the Chapels building. It has some very damaged frescoes at the front; the ones at the top of the building are in better condition.

Medici chapels

The Medici Chapels were started in the sixteenth century. Cardinal Giulio de Medici, one of the four family popes, decided a family mausoleum was needed and asked Michelangelo to build it. Michelangelo also worked on the statues and tombs inside.

Inside you will find there are three distinct areas.

The crypt is rather plain and where they placed most of the lesser known Medici family members – so you can walk through it fairly quickly unless you spot something interesting.

Chapel of the Princes

Inside this spectacular octagonal room you will find the very ostentatious tombs of six of the Medici Grand Dukes and Duchesses. They are Cosimo I, Francesco I, Cosimo II, Ferdinando I, Cosimo III, and Ferdinando II

Each one is interred in a sarcophagus adorned with bronze statues. The room is covered in semi-precious stones and marble, which cost a fortune to construct. They were still building it when the last of the Medicis died, and in fact it was only completed in 1962.

There is one interesting omission – Bianca Capello, who if you remember was the mistress of Francesco I before finally marrying him. The family refused to have her interred in the family chapel when she died, and in fact no-one knows where she is buried. Francesco was actually buried with his first wife Christina of Lorraine.

163

The walls are inlaid with jasper, lapis lazuli, marble, coral, mother of pearl, and agate, all used to display the 16 coats of arms of the cities which were subject to the Grand Duchy

Continue to the New Sacristy,

The New Sacristy

The sacristy is entirely the work of Michelangelo, who built the tombs of two of the Medici.

Night and Day

The first one holds Giuliano, the duke de Nemours, who sits above the statues of Night and Day.

The statue of Night (the female one) is thought to be one of Michelangelo's masterpieces – although you might think Night is rather masculine looking – just like Michelangelo's Virgin Mary you saw in the Uffizi.

Dawn and Dusk

The second tomb holds the grandson of Lorenzo the Magnificent, also called Lorenzo, and sits atop "Dawn" and "Dusk".

You might wonder why Day and Dusk are masculine and Night and Dawn are feminine – it's simply the gender given to the words in Italian – e.g. night is la note

Michelangelo admitted that he purposefully made both Lorenzo and Giuliano much more powerful and impressive than they were in real life. He reportedly said:

> "in 1000 years nobody would remember what they looked like anyway"

Very true. Years later Michelangelo's drawings were discovered hidden in a tiny niche in the Sacristy - you can see them if you go through the little door next to the altar.

So where is Lorenzo the Magnificent's tomb? Good question. Lorenzo and brother Giuliano are also in the Sacristy but almost as an afterthought. They did get a Michelangelo statue above them but it's very low key compared to the rest of the family. Considering that Lorenzo was so important for Florence and the whole Renaissance, it seems very ungrateful.

Exit and turn left to return to the square. Cross it to continue into Via del Giglio. As you do you will pass the Palazzo Gaddi on your right at the corner of Via dell'Amorino.

Palazzo Gaddi

You can see immediately that it has a style quite different to the rest of Florence, and its interior is beautiful. At one time it had a sumptuous garden long since gone which was nicknamed Gaddi's Paradise. The Gaddi family played host to John Milton in the seventeenth century, and it's said that the palazzo and its garden were the inspiration for Paradise Lost.

Via Giglio

Watch out for number eight on your left as you walk down this street. This is the Pension Burchianti one of Florence's most haunted houses – or so the stories tell us. There are supposed to be three ghosts in residence. One of the haunted rooms is where Mussolini stayed whilst visiting Florence – and guests report that they feel watched and cold in that room! The other two ghosts are an old lady and a child.

Continue along Via Giglio passing Via dell'Alloro on your left.

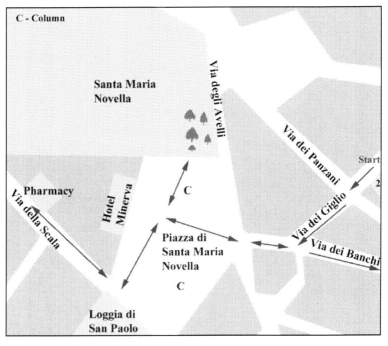

Find number 2 on your left hand side on the next block. You will see a tiny little door to the left of the real door - it's clearly not used to get in and out. It's called a "buchette del vino", and is where the owners of the building sold bottles of wine to the passing public.

You will reach a junction with Via Panzani which you should cross carefully and continue on Via del Giglio. When you reach the junction with Via dei Banchi, turn right to reach Piazza Maria Novella.

Piazza Santa Maria Novella

Before you tackle the Santa Maria Novella, have a look at the square itself. Because of its size this square was used for all sorts of spectacles.

One event was the Pallio dei Cocchi or the Chariot Race, which was started by Cosimo I. The obelisks you see at either end of the square, standing on top of the backs of turtles, used to be turning points for the chariot races which were held here from the sixteenth to the nineteenth century – shame they stopped really.

The church of Santa Maria Novella fills the right hand side. On the opposite side of the square from the Church is the Loggia di San Paolo where the Grand Duke would sit to watch the chariot race. These days it's a photography museum.

If you face the church, the Hotel Minerva is on your left, and there is a plaque on the wall to Longfellow. Longfellow stayed there when he was researching Dante in order to translate the Divine Comedy into English – he was just twenty at the time which is pretty impressive.

Santa Maria Novella

This green and white church was the first of Florence's major churches. You might wonder why it is called "new". Well it was built on top of an older church Santa Maria delle Vigne. Stand at the front and look right to the top to see the two large curved scrolls on either side of the top part of the church. This is the first church to have this type of decoration, but it was immediately popular and you will find it copied all over Italy.

Tombs

At the bottom of the church there is a line of arches each one holding a tomb. The well-off families of Florence would buy a tomb and decorate it with the family coat of arms. If you look down the right hand side of the church Via degli Avelli, you will see them lining the wall all the way down. In fact Via degli Avelli means Tomb Street.

Astronomy

Right at the top of the facade you can see the sun shining brightly - the sun was the symbol of the Convent of Santa Maria Novella. At the bottom on either side you can see two astronomical devices, a bronze armillary sphere on one side and a marble sundial on the other. Both devices were put there at the request of Friar Ignazio Danti.

Fra Danti used them to figure out why the Julian calendar was not quite correct and finally presented his findings to Pope Gregory XIII. This led eventually to the Gregorian calendar which we use today with its built in leap years. When it was adopted, the date was shifted ten days to bring it into line. As a consequence, Saint Theresa of Avila died on the night between 4 October and 15 October 1582!

The entrance is at the front of the church and you will walk through the graveyard to reach the door. Once in the church walk around the interior in a clockwise direction.

The Pulpit

You will reach a marble pulpit – the spot where the church first denounced Galileo and his heretic theories.

Masaccio's 'Holy Trinity'

A little further on you will see this fresco by Masaccio. The church was at one point decorated with frescoes but they were obliterated in the 16th century by order of Cosimo I. This

168

single fresco survived as it was covered only by a painting. It's one of the first examples of painting perspective – where items in the background are painted smaller than the foreground. When it was first on show, visitors would stand and stare in astonishment, unable to understand why the background seemed to recede from their view.

At the foot of the cross is the Virgin Mary, but this time she is not gazing at her son, instead she is looking at you – as if she is saying "do you understand?"

Below Mary is a sarcophagus with an accompanying skeleton. The sarcophagus wall is inscribed in Latin which translates to

"I once was what you are, and what I am you also will be"

Basically it's a warning that we all die eventually.

Cappella Strozzi

Continue towards the end of the church and on your left and up some steps you will find the Strozzi chapel, which is decorated with Dante's Divine Comedy. The last Judgment is on the back wall, hell is on the right and paradise is on the left.

Also on the right wall is the fresco of St Philip Driving the Dragon from the Temple of Hierapolis by Fra Lippi.

The pulpit has beautiful bas-reliefs. The first one shows The Annunciation, and it is lit by a ray of light coming through a stained glass window on March 25, the day of the Annunciation – assuming it's a sunny day of course.

The Green Cloister

This little cloister is through a door on your left as you enter the church and it's well worth a walk round. It gets its name from the green colouring of the wall frescoes.

Grand Cloister

The Grand Cloister is actually owned by the Carabinieri (police force) but it has recently been opened to the public.

Cappella Gaddi

The star of this chapel is Giotto's crucifix. Giotto portrayed the real suffering of Jesus rather than the older Byzantine crucifixion scene.

Capella Gondi

I am sure you remember Brunelleschi the architect of the Cathedral Dome. Well he was also a keen sculptor and you can see one of his rare works here. Apparently he saw Donatello's crucifix in Santa Croce and was a little unimpressed. He thought it primitive and not worthy, so he did his own!

Tornabuoni Chapel

This chapel is full of colourful frescoes. It was under the patronage of the Ricci family, but they went bankrupt in 1348 and so had no money for its upkeep. They wanted to sell their rights to the chapel to the Sassetti family, but the Sassettis wanted to decorate it with frescoes about Saint Francis of Assisi. That didn't go down well with the Dominicans whose church it was so the deal was blocked. The Ricci family finally offloaded it to Giovanni Tornabuoni who had the chapel re-frescoed to what you see now. The artists he gave the commission to had workshops – and one of the apprentices was Michelangelo.

The main picture is the arrival of a new baby – who happened to be the Virgin Mary. Oddly the entire scene has been transposed to a Florentine home!

Spanish chapel

The Spanish Chapel was named after Eleanor of Toledo, the wife of Cosimo I. She gave him eleven children ensuring the family line for a generation at least. The chapel also contains many very colourful frescoes – full of detail. Do take a few minutes to walk in and have a look around.

When you leave the church return to the Piazza and stand between the two obelisks.

If you have any energy left you can visit what is thought to be the oldest pharmacy in the world, the Pharmacy of Santa Maria Novella. If you can't face it, continue from End of Detour a little further on.

To reach the pharmacy stand with the church to your back, then walk forward towards the lovely white colonnaded building in front of you. Turn right into Via della Scala and walk past Via del Porcellana on your left. You will find the Pharmacy of Santa Maria Novella on your right.

Pharmacy of Santa Maria Novella Detour
It started in 1221 and is thought to be the oldest pharmacy in the world. The clever monks from the church you have just visited used their skills to make all sorts of lotions and medicines, and in the seventeenth century started selling them to the public at a healthy profit.

One of their most popular lines long ago was Aceto dei Sette Ladri, or Seven Thieves Vinegar which are smelling salts. The story goes that seven men doused themselves in this concoction and were able to steal from the bodies of plague victims without catching it themselves.

Today the pharmacy still carries some of those products but of course mostly carries modern and luxurious goods.

The building it is in is really beautiful, so go in and wander around and admire the vaulted ceiling, the tasteful glassware, marble floors and statuary. You might even purchase a gift or indulge in a bit of self-indulgence – splash out on a bar of soap!

You can ask about a guided tour when you are in – their web site offers them for free.

When you leave, turn left to return to Piazza Maria Novella and once again stand between the two obelisks.

End of Detour
With the church behind you, turn left to leave the plazza by Via di Banchi.

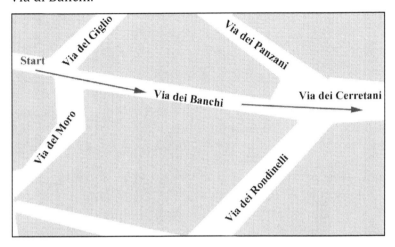

Pass both Via dei Giglio and busy Via dei Panzani on your left. This will take you onto Via dei Cerretani and you will see Via dei Rondinelli on your right.

There is a romantic story attached to that family name. Antonio Rondinelli lived in that street and fell in love with the beautiful Ginevra de Amieri. Sadly her heartless father forced her to marry another man. The plague arrived in Florence and poor Ginevra fell ill, seemingly died, and was buried immediately. However Ginevra was not dead and woke to find herself surrounded by skeletons in the family tomb. She managed to force her way out and returned to her husband's home. He was horrified at the ghost he saw and refused to let her in. Her father had the same reaction, and it was not until she ran to Antonio's home that she was taken in with joy.

Next day at church there was shock all round and her first husband demanded that she come home with him. Ginevra and Antonio appealed to the bishop who said that both husband and father had forfeited all rights to Ginevra. Not only that, the husband had to hand over the dowry to Antonio. It's a great story.

Continue onwards to Piazza di Santa Maria Maggiore and on your right you will see the Santa Maria Maggiore church.

Santa Maria Maggiore

There is a very stumpy church tower at the corner of Via dei Cerretani and Piazza Santa Maria Maggiore. Stand on Via dei Cerretani and look up. Quite high up you should see a small head protruding from the wall.

One legend tells us that a man found guilty of sorcery was being taken to his death at the stake. As he passed the tower a monk leaned out of the tower and shouted warnings to the crowd not to give water to the sorcerer as he would use it to save himself from the flames. The sorcerer immediately cast a spell and turned him to stone!

Another legend tells the story of Berta, the cabbage seller. She was very religious and although not rich she left everything to the church and instructed the monks to buy a bell to be rung before the city gates closed to warn the field workers to return home.

I think the head looks feminine, and Berta's story is the nicer so I believe that legend. Leave Berta and continue along Via dei Cerretani to reach Cathedral Square again and the end of the walk.

Walk 5 - A view across the Arno

This walk takes you across the Arno and up to a wonderful viewpoint. There is far less art to view, so if you have over-dosed, this is a pleasant way to refresh yourself.

You can catch bus 12/13 to avoid the climb but it's not a direct route so you will probably not save much time, just energy. If you want to take the bus consult your bus map to find the nearest stop and then get off at San Miniato al Monte. Pick the route up from San Miniato al Monte below.

Walk up

If you want to walk up, make your way back to Ponte alle Grazie which you didn't cross on Walk 1 and cross the bridge.

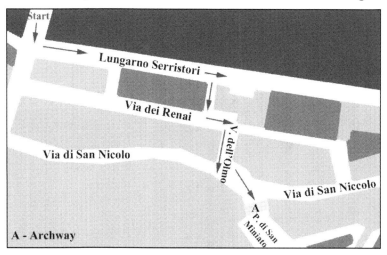

Turn left into Lungarno Serristori to walk along the south bank of the river. Go past a little park on your right. Turn right into Piazza Nicola Demidoff, then left into Via dei Renai. Before the road narrows turn right into Via dell'Olmo, then left into Via di San Niccolò. You will reach a fork in the road so keep right on Via San Miniato. Walk through an archway in the city wall.

City Walls

Florence's city walls have been rebuilt six times, each time the city expanded. The wall you have just walked through is the sixth expansion.

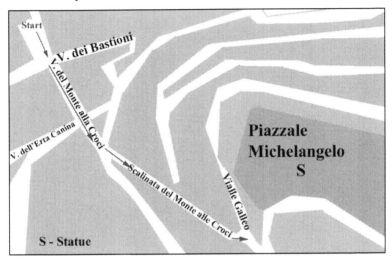

You are now in Piazzetta di San Miniato. Start to climb up Via del Monte alle Croci passing Via dei Bastioni on your left.

Cross the junction with Via dell'Erta Canina on your right. Just a few steps further on you will pass another road coming up from the left. Beyond that point you will reach a fork in the road and see a long flight of steps on your left, this is Via di San Salvatore al Monte. Climb the steps and ignore another set of steps on your left about halfway up. You will reach the top of the hill.

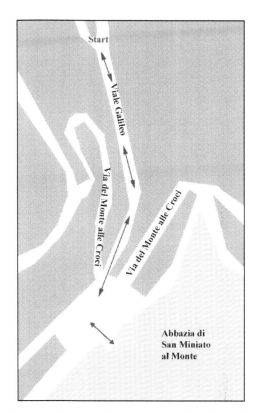

Turn right onto Via Galileo. Ignore the first flight of steps you see on your left; instead walk about 200 yards along tree-lined Viale Galileo to reach a much grander flight of steps also on your left. You have made it!

San Miniato al Monte

The steps will take you up to a green and white marble church, which has been described as the most beautiful church in Italy.

Saint Miniato was in the Roman army, became a Christian, and was hauled up before the Emperor who happened to be camped just outside Florence.

"Feed him to the lions!" said the Emperor, but the lions in the Amphitheatre refused to eat him. "Off with his head!" said the Emperor, but Miniato picked up his decapitated head, put it back on, crossed the Arno, walked to this spot, and became a hermit. Saint Miniato's bones are supposedly in the crypt.

This church was the inspiration for other churches you have visited, including Santa Maria Novella on walk 4 and Santa Croce on walk 1. It went up in 1013 to replace the much older original shrine. It has a bronze eagle at the top, the symbol of the wool merchant's guild who were patrons of the church.

As it lay outside the old city walls it was a prime target to any attacker. The bell-tower was filled with canons used to disrupt the army of the invading Holy Roman Emperor in the sixteenth century – he was trying to return the Medici family to power. Michelangelo suspended mattresses from the tower and managed to save it from the returned fire as the missiles bounced of the mattresses without causing any real harm. However the Medici family eventually did regain power.

Before you go inside, look at the little step at the door. There is an inscription

Which translates as:

This is the gate of heaven

Those were the words uttered by Jacob when he saw the ladder used by the angels to reach God.

Inside it has an unusual marble floor inlaid with the signs of the twelve signs of the Zodiac and an eye-catching elevated pulpit.

There is another old legend regarding Taurus the bull in the pavement. Traditionally, each of the four evangelist saints, Mathew, Mark, Luke, and John has an associated symbol: Man, lion, bull, and eagle. If you look under the pulpit you will see a column with an eagle, a man, a lion, but no bull – so where is Saint Luke? The lions head is turned to gaze at the sign of Taurus in the pavement, alluding to Saint Luke.

Saint Miniato's bones are under the altar, down in the very atmospheric crypt with its beautiful 38 pillars.

The monks, who are still in residence, have a shop which sells liqueurs, honey and herbal teas. Next to the church is the gateway to the cemetery which has many unusual tombstones and statues, so if you have time, take a little walk through it. Carlo Lorenzini who was born in Florence and wrote Pinocchio is buried here.

When you have seen enough descend the church steps back down to Viale Galileo and turn right. Follow this road back to the steps you used to reach Viale Galileo.

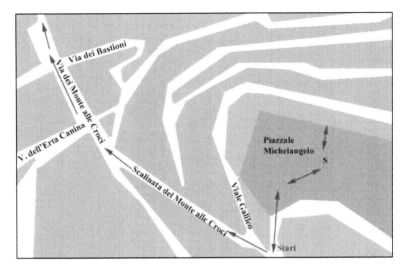

Don't descend straight away. Instead keep straight ahead on the main road and you will soon reach a car park and beyond that Piazzale Michelangelo.

Piazzale Michelangelo

Fittingly there is a copy of David up here watching over Florence. Walk to the terrace edge and let your camera catch the view. You will see the red dome of the Cathedral and the towers of Florence before you. Also make sure you see the old city wall stretch away left and right.

When you have had enough turn to face David then leave the square on your right hand side and walk back along Viale Galileo. You can either take the bus back down to town, or walk.

If you want to walk, cross at the zebra crossing where you will find the steps down the hill again. At the bottom turn right to continue downhill. Walk straight ahead across the junction and go through the archway.

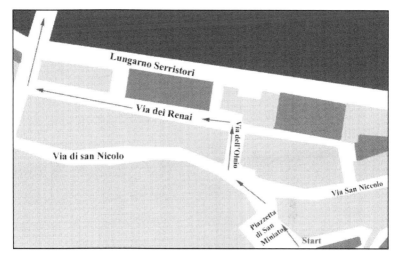

Keep to the main street, Via San Miniato, which will take you into via di San Niccolo. Turn right into Via dell'Olmo and left into Via dei Renai. At the end of this street you will find Museo Bardini on your left, so if you feel you haven't had your daily quota of art, you could pop in.

Museo Bardini

It's a bit of an Aladdin's cave. This is a museum just to wander through and have a look at things which catch your eye.

Bardini was an art collector who bought this building to house it. He even embedded ceilings, doors, windows and other fragments from old buildings into the fabric of the museum. In fact when Florence went on a wrecking spree last century in the Piazza della Repubblica area, he rescued various items and saved them in this building.

He left the entire collection to Florence. It closed in 1999 for an extensive renovation and you can now enjoy the results. The restoration put everything back to the way it was when Bardini died, including the vivid blue wall colours.

On the ground floor there is a sculpture gallery where much loved original works are kept safe and replaced by copies in their original positions - just like Michelangelo's David. Spot the bronze boar which used to stand near the Fontana del Porcellino which you saw on walk 4, the little Devil by Giambologna that adorned the junction between Via dei Vecchietti and Via Strozzi from walk 2, and a golden Marzocco from the Palazzo Vecchio.

There are various ancient Persian rugs on the walls. One exceptionally long one, all 7.5 meters of it, was used when Hitler paid Florence a visit in 1938.

When you exit, turn left and then right to re-cross the bridge and return to town.

Did you enjoy this walk?

I do hope you found this walk both fun and interesting, and I would love feedback. If you have any comments, either good or bad, please review this book. You could also drop me a line on my amazon web page:

Other Tuscan Gems

Tuscany is full of interesting cities and towns; why not visit while you are in Tuscany. Most are just a train ride away from Florence and full of interesting sights:

Printed in Great Britain
by Amazon